FASHION
DESIGN

Required Reading Range
Course Reader

THE
COMPLETE
GUIDE

JOHN HOPKINS

Ethical: aware-
ness/
reflec-
tion/
debate

**a
va**
academia

**TABLE
OF
CONTENTS**

INTRODUCTION

Fashion Design: The Complete Guide presents an illustrated view of fashion design with contexts and definitions, relevant areas of design practice and associated career opportunities.

Fashion can be a notoriously difficult subject to contain, both from an academic point of view and in terms of its changing nature as part of popular culture and contemporary media. The primary aim of this book is to offer current perspectives and insights into the working processes and inter-relationships that exist across the international fashion design industry. In keeping with this outward-facing ethos, the book includes interviews and contributions from selected practitioners, design students and industry professionals, spanning centres of fashion across London, Paris and New York.

This book is designed to assist fashion design students and those aspiring to work in the fashion industry to gain an understanding of the key functions and processes that directly and, sometimes indirectly, inform the critical path from a concept or design theme through to the development and realization of a prototype sample, line or collection. The book is written from a practice-based viewpoint and showcases original artwork and images from a variety of studios.

Each chapter opens with a set of objectives and concludes with discussion questions and suggested activities. It is hoped that these will encourage critical analysis and foster debate in relation to chapter content. In addition, each chapter includes a list of further resources, which acknowledges some of the contributions already made to the broad, yet often specialist areas covered by fashion design, with the opportunity to extend your personal research or critical enquiry through supplementary reading.

Whether you intend to embark on a career as a fashion designer or extend your personal knowledge of the subject, it is hoped that this book will promote and enhance your understanding of fashion design. It is a multifaceted discipline that is capable of accommodating a diversity of thinking and practices linked to aesthetic, industrial, economic and cultural activities and aspirations.

1.0 FASHION IN CONTEXT

OBJECTIVES

To introduce a range of contexts and definitions for fashion

To appreciate different product classifications applicable to fashion design

To consider fashion cycles in relation to seasonal and evolutionary influences

To understand the historical context and emergence of fashion capitals

To recognize the diversity of the international fashion calendar

To begin to critically evaluate fashion in the context of wider media influences

01 — FASHION EDITORIAL
Advertising campaigns and editorial photoshoots continue to offer inspiring and sometimes challenging representations of fashion.
Credit: Anne Combaz for Ponytail magazine

Defining fashion

POPULAR CULTURE

CONTINUOUS CHANGE

Fashion is a multifaceted subject that can be linked to a range of sociological, cultural, psychological and commercial perspectives. Its complex nature makes simplistic definitions of fashion deceptively difficult. While fashion encompasses varying forms of clothing, accessories, lifestyle and behaviour at a given time, 'fashion' remains distinct from 'dress' or 'costume'. A garment does not necessarily represent fashion just because it is a garment. Fashion may therefore be understood in the context of wider contemporary phenomena and human behaviour.

Fashion is widely perceived as operating within the domain of popular culture. Fashion's transitory nature can sometimes make it appear rather trivial. In reality, it requires more detailed analysis and a deeper cultural understanding, with its associations of shared meanings, social interaction and communication channels. Most sociologists and historians agree that culture is learned. In this context, fashion is also learned and constructed as part of a social undertaking that is linked to shared experiences and behaviour. While the motivation to get dressed simply for warmth or protection might be regarded as natural, fashion operates on more complex levels of human engagement and interaction to become a cultural signifier of taste, wealth and aspiration. Fashion's social relationships are further moderated by a combination of individual and collective identities. Fashion culture, then, may broadly be understood as a system that unites individuals, establishes its own rules and offers a social structure in relation to current conditions and societal norms.

Fashion is noted for its continuous cycle of change and revival, which is sometimes linked to the philosophical **zeitgeist** theory. While it is often said that fashion is a reflection of the times, defining what it is to be fashionable is not as straightforward as it may first appear. In order for something to be fashionable it should be contemporarily relevant. Adopting a style that is currently popular offers one simple definition; however, since fashion is inherently evolutionary and continuously redefines itself, the early adopters of fashion are the most likely to be fashionable while at the same time establishing new visual markers for a style or 'look' before mainstream followers adopt the same style or pick up on a trend. In this way the early adopters maintain an impetus for change that defines and redefines fashion but that is moderated by external influences and dominant forces.

Zeitgeist
The term zeitgeist literally means the 'spirit of the times'. Fashion is a component of popular culture and, in accordance with the principles of the zeitgeist, often reflects current political and cultural effects; it is subject to external forces that might include dominant events, ideas, attitudes, social groups and technologies.

Fashion is all about zeitgeist. It has to be something that comes to you, but you have to be like a watch: right on time, because 'zeit' means time. One has to be a well-working Swiss watch. **KARL LAGERFELD**

GENDER

At a fundamental level, fashion is concerned with addressing issues of gender identity, which are commonly defined by social roles and cultural norms. Historically, fashion's association with gender has been informed by age, local customs, status and the relationships between the sexes. In contemporary fashion culture, expressions of gender are increasingly subject to wider media influences and the communication of fashion imagery. From a commercial perspective, womenswear is dominant in comparison to menswear, which still harbours associations of utility and occupational dressing. This imbalance raises further questions about gender relationships with fashion. Gender roles in contemporary fashion may offer an explicit or more ambiguous view of dressing, with terms such as 'boyfriend-fit' entering the fashion vocabulary, while the relationship between modesty and attraction remains culturally defined and explored by many fashion designers.

01

02

01 _ JEAN-PAUL GAULTIER AW11
Androgynous male model Andrej Pejic wears a James Bond-inspired suit for French designer Jean-Paul Gaultier. Pejic also featured in Gaultier's advertising campaign as a female muse.
Credit: Catwalking

02 _ GAULTIER COUTURE SS11
Andrej Pejic wears a bridal gown in Jean-Paul Gaultier's Paris couture show. Pejic's appeal has been linked to fashion's recurring interest with androgyny.
Credit: Catwalking

SOCIAL AND PSYCHOLOGICAL FUNCTIONS

While fashion may appear to present itself at face value, in reality the way we dress affects the way most of us feel about ourselves and the way in which we wish to be viewed by others on a number of social and psychological levels. There remains a distinct social pressure to conform to gender and cultural norms, but fashion is also capable of addressing individual aspirations and identity. Fundamental to fashion design is the shifting representation of the human form and the fashionable body. Examining the ways in which silhouettes have changed throughout history offers a striking visual record of the ideal body at a given time in relation to gender differences and aesthetic ideals. For example, the notion of dressing for comfort is a very modern phenomenon in the history of fashion: arguably the twentieth century's most enduring legacy has been the arrival of sportswear. The notion of being liberated from rules of dressing is countered by the psychological pressures of buying into fashion, either as a signifier of taste or to conform to peer pressures. Either way, fashion remains enduringly contradictory and endlessly fascinating.

TRANSFER OF MEANING

Historically, clothing and dress are associated with the use of symbolism and meanings to construct identities, confirm status and create social and cultural differences or affiliations. This includes the use of decoration and adornment as well as religious or political dress. Clothing can be used to express a collective identity, through modes of dress such as uniform or sportswear. The meanings and associations of dress are frequently adopted and reinterpreted: men's military dress, for example, has become a recurring fashion influence for womenswear that is loaded with associations of meaning but is largely devoid of its original purpose. From a fashion design context, the transfer of meaning also has the capacity to incorporate cross-cultural influences and group affiliations. Sometimes meanings are deliberately subverted and adopted as a symbol of rebellion before entering fashion through a collective consciousness that we might refer to as street style.

ECONOMICS

The fashion industry operates on different levels to service a range of business opportunities aimed at a target consumer audience. The industry is organized across a variety of economic sectors that span national and political boundaries. Thanks to a series of successive industrial and technological advances, which have accelerated since the nineteenth century, the fashion industry is now a multi-linked network that connects production and manufacturing sources to sections of the retail and media industries. One of the most defining aspects of the fashion design industry is the **supply chain**. Efficient management of business supply chains has led to questions and criticisms about a range of social, ethical and environmental issues as well as the **planned obsolescence** on which the supply chain relies to renew itself.

Supply chain
The supply chain is a series of critically planned and sequenced stages by which raw goods are converted into manufactured products and presented for sale or promotion.

Planned obsolescence
Brooks Stevens, who popularized the phrase in 1954, defines it as 'instilling in the buyer the desire to own something a little newer, a little better, a little sooner than is necessary'.

When society produces too much, we invent rituals to get rid of the surplus... we ritually kill fashion by the sale and then await the new hope that comes after. As soon as there's surplus, there will be fashion. **OTTO VAN BUSCH**

01 — EXPLORING IDENTITY
The appropriation of male style and dress has become an accepted influence for womenswear in the context of contemporary fashion. *Credit: Anne Combaz for* Tush *magazine*

HISTORIC TIMELINE OF FASHION

THE MIDDLE AGES

European society organizes itself into royal courts

Christianity influences European dress styles for men and women from the eighth century

Tunic styles evolve into more complex forms with shaping and decoration

Trade and craft skills organized into guilds

Dress styles regulated by sumptuary laws

Fur worn by nobility

Increased tendency towards cutting and shaping of clothes

Introduction of the cote-hardie, a tunic style for men and women

Tippets and hanging sleeves are fashionable

Introduction of the houppelande, an outer gown for men with full body and flared sleeves

Court of Burgundy influences other court styles in Europe

Increased use of silks include new brocades and damasks

THE RENAISSANCE

Regional differences emerge between Italian and northern European Renaissance styles

Widespread fashion for 'slashing' to reveal elaborate undergarments

Shorter-fitting styles more popular in Italy

Men's doublet worn as visible outer garment, jerkins also added

Men's hose divides between padded trunk hose and lower nether hose

Padding techniques develop and greatly influence the fashion silhouette

Laced bodices for women become more rigid as skirts become wider and fuller

A 'pair of bodies' develops as a stiffened, form-fitting bodice, an early form of corset for women

Whalebone stiffeners and centre-front busks are added to the stiffened bodice

Petticoat skirts worn with stiffened bodices under elaborate over-dresses

Fabrics become increasingly ornate for the nobility

Spanish Farthingale, a hooped skirt, worn at court by women

Wearing of severe black made popular by Spanish court for men and women

Fashion for neck ruffs

The drum-shaped Great Farthingale replaces Spanish Farthingale

Unnatural proportions for men and women predominate

Elaborate 'clockwork' and blackwork embroideries become popular

'Peascod belly' doublets and capes become fashionable for men

02-03 —
RENAISSANCE
Queen Elizabeth I wears a Farthingale. Many dress styles of the period distorted the human figure and were stiff and heavy.

01 — MIDDLE AGES
Gothic medieval dress styles saw refinements in weaving and emphasized height and exaggerated proportions.

04 _ BAROQUE

Baroque styles moved towards softer lines and fabrics for a naturalistic appearance, with ornate trims.

04

BAROQUE

As political power in Europe moves from Spain to France, French styles gain influence

Ribbons and laces become popular for men and women

A fuller, more rounded female form becomes fashionable

Waistlines rise

Additional layers of petticoat skirts are worn by women

Lace collars and trims become popular for men and women

Satins and taffetas replace heavy brocades and stiffened fabrics for women

Puritans favour black clothing without decoration

Cavalier-style leather boots with spurs become fashionable for men

Stays (early corsets) are worn by women under basque bodices

French and English courts introduce a new, longer-fitting coat called a cassock/casaque, worn with a long waistcoat. It soon replaces the doublet

Elaborate wigs become fashionable for men

Bodices lengthen and narrow for women as skirt layers persist; some are split at the front

Tricorne hats and buckled shoes become popular for men

Justacorps style added to men's coats as evolution of the cassock/casaque

ROCOCO TO REVOLUTION

Cotton mills set up in France and England to meet popular demand for cotton fabrics. Textile looms also advance

Supporting undergarments include hoops and paniers to accentuate the width of skirts

Move away from heavy masculine proportions to more delicate styles and colours

Trade links with the Far East see the introduction of oriental styles and Chinoiserie, with lighter colours and floral patterns

Frockcoat styles introduced for men

English riding habit and country styles become fashionable for men and women

Sack-back gowns, also called Watteau gowns, become popular in France

Dresses inspired by milk-maidens, shepherdesses and romantic country styles are widely adopted in France

French Revolution repeals sumptuary laws in France, social dress distinctions officially abolished

Revolutionaries call for 'sans culottes' (without knee breeches)

Loose-fitting bridge trousers based on English sailor pants introduced by French revolutionaries

Wigs rapidly go out of fashion

1.0 FASHION IN CONTEXT

05—06 _ ROCOCO

Dress styles during the Rococo years complemented the elegant furnishing and interiors of the period. Men's styles became slimmer and gradually less ostentatious.

05

06

DIRECTOIRE TO ROMANTIC

Extreme dress proportions emerge in post-revolutionary France thanks to the fashion subcultures the Incroyables and Merveilleuses

Cutaway frockcoats evolve into tailcoats for men

Double-breasted tailcoat styles and pantaloons introduced for men

Classically inspired and proportioned dresses based on Ancient Greco-Roman styles are introduced for women. Corsets are abandoned

Waistline returns to natural position, women's undergarments include pantalettes

Demi-corsets introduced

Sleeves increase in size as waists narrow with corsets reintroduced for women

Bonnets become fashionable for women

Neck cravats become essential dress for gentlemen

Beau Brummell adapts English country styles to the gentleman's wardrobe

NINETEENTH CENTURY

Men's dress styles become dominated by sober colours such as black, navy and grey

Women's silhouette expands with introduction of crinoline foundations

Zouave jacket and Garibaldi shirt styles introduced for women

Corset shaping becomes more refined with new technology

Charles Frederick Worth establishes his eponymous haute couture house in Paris

Foundations of Savile Row tailoring traditions in London

Sewing machines are introduced, which increase the manufacture and production of clothing

English sporting styles include Norfolk style and sack jackets cut in sporting tweeds

Black- and white-tie protocols established for men's formal attire

Lounge jacket introduced as daywear for men

Bustles introduced for women

Close-fitting cuirass bodice emphasizes narrow-waist silhouette for women with wide, leg-of-mutton sleeves

Four-in-hand neck tie introduced for men

Princess-line bodices and gored skirts emphasize a graceful, narrow-waisted silhouette

02 — NINETEENTH CENTURY
The domestic role of women was defined through the restraining corsets and expanding full-length skirts.

01 — DIRECTOIRE
The French Revolution had a profound impact on dress styles. For men, a new sobriety emerged in more restrained colours.

TWENTIETH CENTURY

Paris hosts world's fair in 1900 with a fashion pavilion to promote haute couture

Female silhouette dominated by S-shape corset and 'pouter pigeon' chest

Paul Poiret opens his own couture house and is influenced by orientalism

Straighter silhouette emerges for women with Empire line revival

Driving and duster coat styles become popular for men and women

Military influences cross over into fashion for men and women

Hemlines rise significantly for women; pale stockings introduced

Flapper style and men's sporting clothes influence womenswear

Coco Chanel and Elsa Schiaparelli become the most influential couturiers in Paris

Hollywood glamour influences fashion

World War II sees the temporary closure of Paris couture houses

In 1947 Dior presents highly influential 'New Look' collection and re-establishes Paris's reputation

Dior, Chanel and Balenciaga lead Paris fashion in the mid-twentieth century

New generation of easy-care fabrics accelerates rise of sportswear

Women's silhouette moves from fitted lines to straighter, more youthful line

Miniskirts for women introduced in the 1960s as part of pop culture influences

Ready-to-wear designer clothing lines introduced by Paris couture houses

Trouser suits popularized for women and more relaxed dress styles dominate in the 1970s

Shoulder pads and power dressing adopted by men and women in the 1980s

Extended fashion lines service all levels of the fashion market

Fashion enters digital age: rise of e-tailing, blogs and mobile communication

03

03 — TWENTIETH CENTURY
The twentieth century saw the emancipation of women from restrictive corsets and a new-found confidence exemplified by early screen stars such as Clara Bow.

The fashion system

COUTURE

Fashion design operates as part of a structured, international fashion industry. Industrial and technological advances have directly contributed to increasingly efficient supply chains, with each business fulfilling a price category to serve a fashion retail segment. In the fashion industry, the method of production usually provides an early indicator to the type of business and target market. When conceptualized as a hierarchical model, the fashion industry can be viewed as follows:

Couture (haute couture): unique designs made to couture standards from leading names including Chanel and Christian Dior.

Designer: top designer ready-to-wear lines such as Dries Van Noten, Yohji Yamamoto and Prada.

Bridge or diffusion: more moderately priced lines that 'bridge' the gap between 'designer' and 'better' categories, such as Marc by Marc Jacobs, DKNY and Emporio Armani.

Upper high street: good-quality branded labels and private labels sold through a variety of chains and retail outlet labels, including Karen Millen, LK Bennett and Jones New York.

Mid-high street: this category includes contemporary and private labels with competitively priced fashion-forward merchandise, such as Gap, Express and Next.

Lower high street: volume-selling merchandise that is moderately priced and might include adaptations of higher priced merchandise categories. Examples include H&M and New Look.

Budget: mass-produced goods at very affordable price points. Includes supermarket and mass merchandise private labels such as Primark and Cherokee (sold through Tesco in the UK and Target in the USA).

Couture refers to unique or exclusive designs that are made for individual clients. Since its inception in the nineteenth century, couture has become synonymous with the highest standards of quality and service, underscored by highly skilled labour processes. In France, couture is officially known as haute couture and protected under law. Since 1945, the criteria for haute couture membership has been defined and updated by the Chambre Syndicale de la Haute Couture. Spanning clothing, jewellery and accessories, an haute couture establishment is required to adhere to strict membership criteria that include maintaining at least one workshop in Paris, known as an atelier, and employing at least 15 full-time technical staff. Additional criteria require the clothes to be entirely made-to-measure for clients without pre-cutting or assembling and for couturiers to present their collections twice a year. Chanel and Dior maintain the two largest couture houses in Paris today. While haute couture represents the pinnacle of fashion design, financially the couture system relies on additional income sources that include perfume licensing and ready-to-wear designer lines, known in France as prêt-à-porter. In Italy, with its history of craftsmanship, couture is known as alta moda and centred in Rome rather than Milan. London and New York have a small number of establishments that might be considered on a par with couture; however, Paris remains the undisputed global centre for couture.

Bespoke tailoring for men, also known as custom tailoring, offers a comparable service to couture that includes personal fittings as well as hand cutting and finishing by highly skilled tailors in specialized work rooms. London's Savile Row is the most famous centre for bespoke tailoring in the world.

Savile Row
Savile Row is a shopping street in Mayfair, central London, famous for its traditional men's bespoke tailoring. The term bespoke is understood to have originated in Savile Row when cloth for a suit was said to 'be spoken for' by individual customers. The street is known as the golden mile of tailoring. Customers to Savile Row over the years have included Winston Churchill, Lord Nelson and Napoleon III.

**01 — SAAB HAUTE
COUTURE AW10**
Elie Saab is invited by
the Chambre Syndicale
de la Haute Couture
in Paris to present his
eponymous couture
collections. The
Beruit-born designer
is inspired by a mix of
Eastern and Western
influences.
Credit: Catwalking

**02 — DIOR HAUTE
COUTURE AW10**
Dior couture
shows have been
extravagant
presentations in
recent years. Such
shows promote
and validate the
label's position as a
leading global luxury
brand across all its
associated lines.
Credit: Catwalking

READY-TO-WEAR

Adapted from the French term prêt-à-porter, ready-to-wear clothing originally referred to 'off-the-peg' designer clothing lines that were manufactured to commercially high standards against pre-determined size scales at relatively affordable price points. Introduced during the 1960s, ready-to-wear was a commercial imperative for some of the ailing couture houses and the links to an established couture name made the original ready-to-wear collections highly marketable. Over the years, however, the term ready-to-wear has become widely used and more generic as the fashion retail sector continues to expand and diversify into a variety of private labels and wholesale brands. Today ready-made clothing includes mass-produced lines across a broad range of pricing categories.

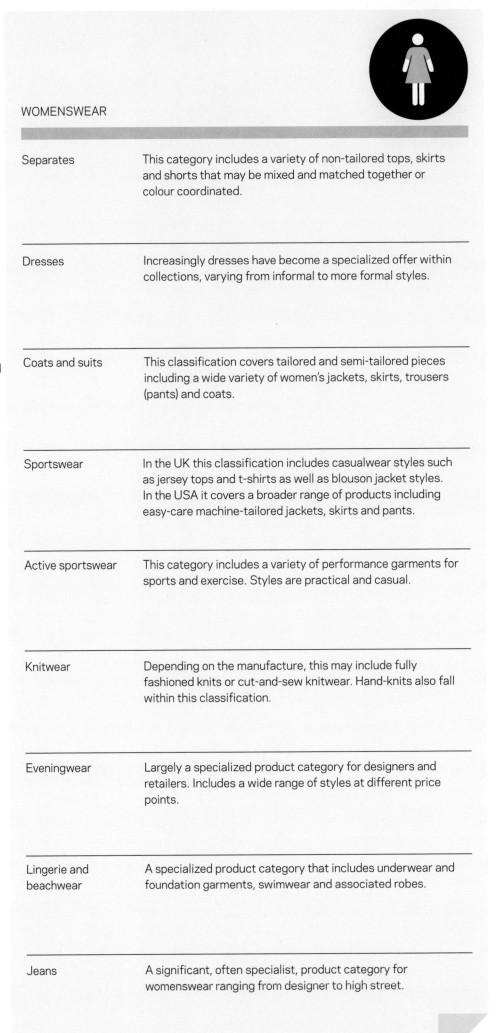

WOMENSWEAR

Separates	This category includes a variety of non-tailored tops, skirts and shorts that may be mixed and matched together or colour coordinated.
Dresses	Increasingly dresses have become a specialized offer within collections, varying from informal to more formal styles.
Coats and suits	This classification covers tailored and semi-tailored pieces including a wide variety of women's jackets, skirts, trousers (pants) and coats.
Sportswear	In the UK this classification includes casualwear styles such as jersey tops and t-shirts as well as blouson jacket styles. In the USA it covers a broader range of products including easy-care machine-tailored jackets, skirts and pants.
Active sportswear	This category includes a variety of performance garments for sports and exercise. Styles are practical and casual.
Knitwear	Depending on the manufacture, this may include fully fashioned knits or cut-and-sew knitwear. Hand-knits also fall within this classification.
Eveningwear	Largely a specialized product category for designers and retailers. Includes a wide range of styles at different price points.
Lingerie and beachwear	A specialized product category that includes underwear and foundation garments, swimwear and associated robes.
Jeans	A significant, often specialist, product category for womenswear ranging from designer to high street.

MENSWEAR

Jeans	Jeans have become a significant product category of menswear from designer and brand labels to budget labels available across a range of fits.
Casualwear	Large sector for menswear, aimed primarily at the youth market. Heavily branded category that covers a variety of merchandise including t-shirts, hoodies, casual pants and shirt styles.
Active sportswear	Heavily branded for men and closely linked to athletic footwear, this product category distinguishes itself from casualwear by featuring technical fabrics designed for a range of athletic activities.
Knitwear	Branded knitwear dominates for menswear and is available across a range of categories, from fully fashioned and cut-and-sew to hand-knits.
Tailored clothing	An important category for menswear that includes tailored suits, jackets, coats, trousers, shirts and neck ties. Merchandise quality can vary considerably depending on the market level and manufacturing processes involved.
Formalwear	Specialist category usually related to tailored clothing. Includes tuxedos and dinner suits with male accessories such as bow ties and cummerbunds.
Outerwear	Broad category of products that includes non-tailored coat styles such as parka coats and padded jackets as well as three-quarter length coats. Includes branded merchandise.
Rainwear and coats	Competition from the outerwear sector has seen rainwear become more specialist or seasonal within some collections. Traditionally this category included full-length styles that are more formal than outerwear.

LICENSING

Ready-made clothing lines are sometimes designed and manufactured under licence. Licensing involves an agreement between an established fashion company and a manufacturer whereby the name and logo of the fashion label may be used to produce additional product lines. In this way a fashion label may be able to extend its product offer into a specialist category such as swimwear, or penetrate an export market by utilizing local knowledge and expertise in return for an agreed royalty fee. All licensing agreements need to be carefully managed to ensure that the brand or label is not devalued or that a market is not saturated with one product or style.

FASHION CYCLES

Fashion is frequently associated with seasonal trends. In the context of fashion design this may be understood as a dominant 'look' or prevailing style or colour that give rise to a sense of collective dressing at a given time. The visual impact of collective dressing might prompt a defining silhouette for men or women. This is usually informed by a shift in body proportions or the introduction of a new shape that might be defined by the cut of a jacket or coat. The process is further informed and supported by media communication channels including fashion and style magazines, advertising and the Internet. The changing nature of fashion combined with the zeitgeist theory ensures that fashion or 'being fashionable' does not exist in a state of suspension or permanence. Fashion and styles change over time in response to a mix of external and social influences or stimuli, so that being 'in fashion' becomes transitory. The fashion industry is not a passive bystander in this regard but is motivated by a range of commercial interests towards supporting continuous seasonal changes that, over time, may be viewed as cyclical stages.

01—04 _ ANNA SUI AW11
Fashion designers will often seek inspiration from previous decades, which may include updating a look or style for a contemporary audience. This approach will only succeed if the designs are relevant to the times so that they do not appear as costume. Designer Anna Sui is highly skilled in researching and updating looks for her collections.

01

1.0 FASHION IN CONTEXT

04

STAGES IN THE FASHION CYCLE

The notion of fashion as a transitory condition is often expressed through fashion cycles. There are three main cycles: the fad, the standard trend cycle and the classic cycle. A fad is a short-lived cycle; the standard cycle represents a fuller seasonal cycle and the classic cycle is more prolonged, within which a style endures beyond seasonal trends.

Each cycle may be measured through a series of stages according to timescale. Stage 1 represents the introduction of a style. During this early stage fashion-forward consumers, also known as early adopters, start to wear a new style, which can receive mixed reactions from others. Stage 2 is the rise. During this stage the style gains wider acceptance and is usually promoted through media and advertising channels. Fashion followers pick up on the style as it gains wider acceptance, extending the style's profile and appeal. Stage 3 represents the peak of a style's popularity when it is said to enter maturity. By this stage the style is widely adopted across all market levels and, at its peak, will reach saturation point, when the majority of consumers have accepted it, often in modified forms. Most fashion-forward consumers will have dropped the style by this time. Stage 4 is the decline stage. During this stage the style may be widely worn by less style-conscious consumers and appears over-exposed. It may be discounted by retailers and is worn by a declining number of fashion followers. Stage 5 is referred to as obsolescence. By this stage the style is firmly 'out of fashion' or so over-exposed that it looks dated or like a poor imitation of the original style.

In a fad cycle, a style will rapidly move from stages 1 to 5 through an accelerated process. Most fads are the result of over-exposure or a rapid saturation in the market. The standard trend cycle represents more of a fashion industry model whereby a style is accepted over a seasonal timescale and may be revived in the future, although not in its original form. The classic cycle is less of a cycle than either a fad or standard trend cycle since it does not enter the obsolescence stage. Products within this cycle may be basics or staple items. These tend to be modified over the years and are usually associated with utility or functionality.

In a global economy the challenges and changes are universal.

ROBERT HELLER

01

02

03

01-03 — FASHION CYCLES
These diagrams illustrate the three main cycles in fashion: the fad cycle, the standard trend cycle and the classic cycle.

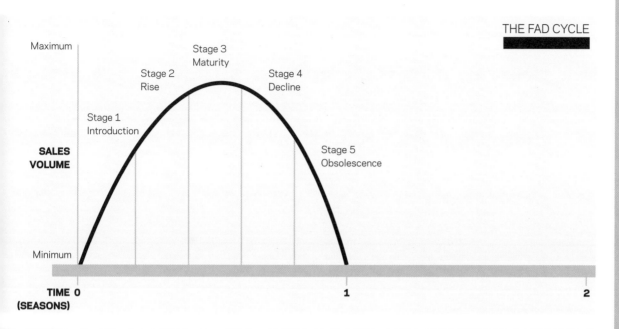

THE FAD CYCLE

Maximum

Stage 3
Maturity

Stage 2
Rise

Stage 4
Decline

Stage 1
Introduction

Stage 5
Obsolescence

**SALES
VOLUME**

Minimum

TIME   0   1   2
(SEASONS)

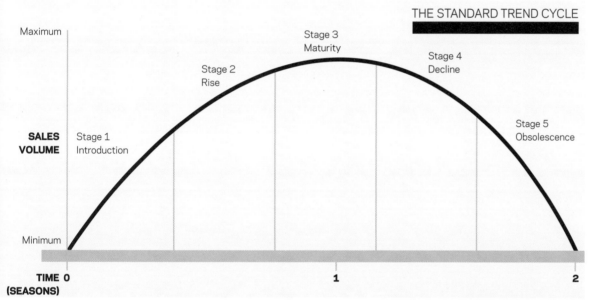

THE STANDARD TREND CYCLE

Maximum

Stage 3
Maturity

Stage 2
Rise

Stage 4
Decline

Stage 1
Introduction

Stage 5
Obsolescence

**SALES
VOLUME**

Minimum

TIME   0   1   2
(SEASONS)

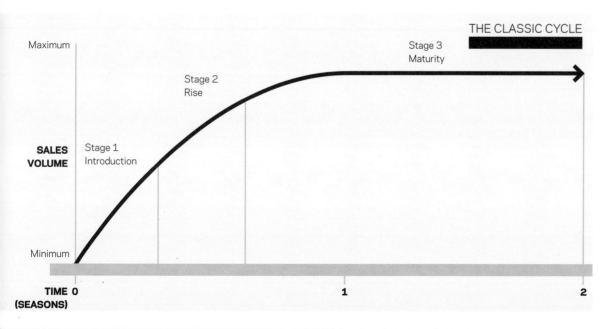

THE CLASSIC CYCLE

Maximum

Stage 3
Maturity

Stage 2
Rise

Stage 1
Introduction

**SALES
VOLUME**

Minimum

TIME   0   1   2
(SEASONS)

THE FASHION CALENDAR

The growth of the commercial ready-to-wear exhibition reflects the international diversification of the fashion industry. Fashion week events have proliferated over the past decade to include over 30 countries. While it would be impossible to list all the events here, what follows is a calendar of the world's main trade fairs and fashion weeks.

NAME	LOCATION + DATE	WEBSITE	DESCRIPTION
Atmosphère's	Paris March October	www.pretparis.com	Selection of emerging and directional premium labels. The Paris show attracts international buyers attending Paris Fashion Week.
Berlin Fashion Week	Berlin January July	www.mbfashionweek.com	German and international designers and premium brands present their catwalk collections at this exhibition event in Berlin.
The Brandery	Barcelona January July	www.thebrandery.com	Contemporary womenswear, young designers and streetwear are all represented at this trade show, which is attended by international buyers.
Bread and Butter	Berlin January July	www.breadandbutter.com	Denim labels, streetwear, urbanwear and a variety of niche labels are represented at this trade show held in Berlin's Tempelhof airport.
Copenhagen International Fashion Fair	Copenhagen February August	www.ciff.dk	Showcase for Scandinavian fashion and mainstream European womenswear brands. Includes a combination of catwalk presentations and exhibitor shows.
CPH Vision	Copenhagen February August	www.cphvision.dk	Contemporary womenswear and directional labels focusing on Scandinavian design. The event is held in conjunction with Terminal 2, a streetwear and denim show.
The Exhibition at London Fashion Week	London February September	www.londonfashionweek.co.uk	Contemporary fashion and accessories offered from established designers and niche womenswear labels. Held in conjunction with the London Fashion Week catwalk shows.
Fashion Coterie	New York February September	www.enkshows.com	High-end womenswear brands presented in conjunction with footwear event Sole Commerce. Attended by buyers from department stores and independent boutiques seeking premium ready-to-wear collections.
Fashion Mavericks	London February September	www.fashionmavericks.com	Fashion shows and an open space for new and independent designers to exhibit directional womenswear collections. Held at the same time as London Fashion Week.
Intersélection	Paris April November	www.interselection.net	Ready-to-wear trade show includes accessories collections for multiple retailers and mid-market brands. The exhibition links designers, manufacturers and retailers.
Living Room Tokyo	Tokyo March October	www.livingroomtokyo.com	Innovative and directional designer collections are presented alongside trend-led accessories. Living Room takes place during Japan Fashion Week.

NAME	LOCATION + DATE	WEBSITE	DESCRIPTION
London Fashion Week	London February September	www.londonfashionweek.co.uk	London's premier fashion design event showcases a mix of established labels and emerging talent and it has a reputation for creativity and design innovation. London Fashion Week includes a dedicated men's day.
Los Angeles Fashion Market	Los Angeles March August	www.californiamarketcenter.com	Key show for West Coast ready-to-wear and streetwear labels in conjunction with kidswear and footwear shows.
Los Angeles Majors Market	Los Angeles April October	www.californiamarketcenter.com	Large number of young fashion ranges from denim to contemporary labels aimed at multiple retailers and department store buyers.
Magic	Las Vegas	www.magiconline.com	Contemporary menswear and womenswear show attracting domestic and international buyers looking for American labels.
Margin	London February November	www.margin.tv	Niche and directional labels for men and women are offered to buyers at this London exhibition. Intended as a launch pad for new designers.
Milan Fashion Week	Milan February September	www.cameramoda.it	Milan's premier event to showcase top womenswear designers including Prada and Gucci to international buyers and press. Milan Fashion Week is a highlight in the fashion calendar and is attended by international buyers and celebrities.
Milan Men's Fashion Week	Milan January June	www.cameramoda.it	Milan's premier event to showcase top menswear labels to international buyers and press.
Milanovendemoda	Milan February September	www.milanovendemoda.it	Well-established ready-to-wear exhibition for womenswear and accessories representing over 200 contemporary Italian brands.
Moda Manhattan	New York February August	www.modamanhattan.com	Contemporary ready-to-wear collections from occasion-wear to sportswear are included in this New York exhibition. Held in conjunction with the Accessories Show to attract buyers and retailers.
New York Fashion Week	New York February September	www.mbfashionweek.com	New York's premier fashion event to showcase top womenswear fashion labels, including Marc Jacobs and Ralph Lauren, to international buyers and press. New York Fashion Week is a highlight in the fashion calendar and is attended by international buyers and celebrities.
On/Off	London February September	www.onoff.tv	Running alongside London Fashion Week, On/Off has become an important showcase for breaking new talent through catwalk and exhibition events.

NAME	LOCATION + DATE	WEBSITE	DESCRIPTION
Paris Fashion Week	Paris March October	www.modeaparis.com	Paris Fashion Week is the premier fashion event for top ready-to-wear womenswear fashion labels including Louis Vuitton, Chanel and Lanvin. Paris Fashion Week is a highlight in the fashion calendar and is attended by international buyers and celebrities.
Paris Haute Couture	Paris January July	www.modeaparis.com	Exclusive womenswear collections made to rigorous standards from the most prestigious Parisian fashion houses, including Chanel and Christian Dior. Attended by invited clients and press only.
Paris Men's Fashion Week	Paris January June	www.modeaparis.com	Selection of top international designers, including Louis Vuitton, Paul Smith and Dior Homme, present their ready-to-wear collections to buyers and press.
Pitti Immagine Uomo	Florence January June	www.pittimmagine.com	Key menswear fair for showcasing mainstream and contemporary menswear. Pitti Immagine Uomo combines clothing and accessories from tailoring houses with lifestyle brands and emerging labels.
Pitti Immagine W	Florence January June	www.pittimmagine.com	Premium womenswear brands present their pre-collections at this show.
Prêt à Porter Paris	Paris January October	www.pretparis.com	Contemporary and cutting-edge womenswear labels are presented as part of this large Parisian fashion fair. Prêt includes So Ethnic for sustainable fashion labels.
Project	New York & Las Vegas February August	www.projectshow.com	Held biannually in New York and Las Vegas, Project showcases contemporary boutique brands alongside sportswear and high-end denim labels. It attracts international buyers seeking new American brands.
Pure London	London February August	www.purelondon.com	Broad range of contemporary womenswear, streetwear and accessories labels offered as part of a trade show aimed at contemporary and mainstream markets.
Pure Spirit	London February August	www.purelondon.com	Trend-led men's and women's collections presented and offered in conjunction with Pure London exhibition.
Rendez-Vous Femme	Paris March October	www.rendez-vous-paris.com	As part of Paris Fashion Week, Rendez-Vous Femme offers a platform to contemporary, niche and innovative designer brands. Attracts indie and department store buyers looking to discover emerging design talent and brands.
Rendez-Vous Homme	Paris January June	www.rendez-vous-paris.com	Rendez-Vous Homme offers a platform to contemporary, niche and innovative menswear brands from its venue in the Marais district of Paris.

NAME	LOCATION + DATE	WEBSITE	DESCRIPTION
Simm Madrid	Madrid February September	www.simm.ifema.es	Madrid's showcase event for ready-to-wear collections and a limited selection of menswear and lingerie.
Stitch	London February	www.stitchmenswear.com	Dedicated menswear trade show with ready-to-wear and accessories from established and emerging labels. Includes menswear categories across four themed areas: denim, edge, energy and vision.
The Train	New York February September	www.thetrainnewyork.com	Located in the historic Terminal Warehouse building in New York City's Chelsea, The Train offers mainly American premium and niche brands to international buyers in an upscale environment.
Tranoi Femme	Paris March October	www.tranoi.com	High-end contemporary womenswear collections and directional brands are presented at Tranoi four times a year to coincide with Paris Fashion Week. Attracts boutique buyers.
Tranoi Homme	Paris January June	www.tranoi.com	Held four times a year, Tranoi Homme showcases contemporary menswear collections and directional brands.
White Donna	Milan February September	www.whiteshow.it	Contemporary womenswear show that attracts international buyers and retailers attending Milan Fashion Week.
White Homme	Milan January August	www.whiteshow.it	Contemporary and directional menswear show that attracts buyers attending Milan Men's fashion Week. Known for its directional catwalk shows and creative atmosphere.
Who's Next	Paris January September	www.whosnext.com	A wide range of new and established contemporary brands for men and women spanning urban and denim to designer collections arranged in different zones.

Fashion capitals

COURT INFLUENCE

PARIS

Fashion has become synonymous with geographic locations, sometimes referred to as fashion capitals. Historically in Europe the earliest centres of fashion were defined through the royal courts with the reigning monarch or high nobility dictating the accepted dress styles and protocols of the day. Status and displays of wealth were central to early expressions of what passed for fashion, while sumptuary laws maintained and reinforced social distinctions.

The link between fashion and a court's political and economic influence was recognized by competing nations as a form of cultural hegemony. During the sixteenth century, Spain asserted itself as Europe's dominant political and military power while at the same time propagating its formal court dress styles to other European courts. This included very ornate, structured textiles and rigid modes of dress, most notably the Spanish Farthingale for women and the fashion for wearing severe black. By the seventeenth century, however, France had replaced Spain as Europe's pre-eminent political power, ushering in the Baroque era. Dress styles took on a more colourful, theatrical and often passionate expression. From this period, France and particularly Paris established itself as a fashion capital, a position that it has never really lost. Under the long reign of King Louis XIV, France systematically promoted and exported French dress styles based on unyielding artistic rules and a closed view of French society.

The French Revolution of the late eighteenth century briefly halted France's political ambitions and its cultural dominance of dress styles in Europe, enabling the simpler, more 'natural' styles from England to be adopted. This included variations on English riding costumes for men and women, which greatly influenced the development of fashion during the early nineteenth century. Tailoring techniques advanced considerably during this period as some of the best English tailors established their workshops around Savile Row, in London, and England defined its position as a centre for high-quality menswear.

The establishment of haute couture in Paris reinstated its position as the pre-eminent centre for women's fashion in Europe. Paris dominated women's fashion in a way that may seem difficult to imagine today. The establishment of Parisian couture houses led to a system of dominance in fashion that was unrivalled until the Second World War. Publications such as *Gazette du Bon Ton* propagated the authority of Paris fashion and until the outbreak of war, Paris's unique position seemed unassailable. The Second World War temporarily halted the export of Paris fashion to overseas markets including the United States. Paris forcefully reasserted its status as a fashion tour de force, with the immediate impact of Christian Dior's landmark collection '**The New Look**'.

The New Look
On 12 February 1947, Dior launched his first fashion collection for spring/summer. He presented a collection of luxurious clothes with soft shoulders, cinched waists and mid-length full skirts. Initially controversial for using such large quantities of fabric when rationing was still in place, it was in fact absolutely appropriate for the post-war era: women wanted to wear something new after years of brutality and hardship.

01 — LONDON FASHION WEEK
London Fashion Week is a leading event in the fashion calendar with a reputation for showcasing new and emerging design talent. It has also recognized the increasing influence of digital media and was the first major fashion week to offer live-stream broadcasts of designer collections online.
Credit: Farrukh Younus @Implausibleblog

USA

ITALY

Hollywood began to influence popular styles during the 1920s and 30s and the USA was beginning to produce some notable designers of its own. This period signalled the emergence of the United States as a global influence, with New York as its fashion capital. American designer Claire McCardell led the way by rejecting the formalities and dictates of Paris. In doing so, McCardell asserted an all-American look that we would recognize today as the foundations of modern sportswear. Pioneering the concept of separates, McCardell went on to influence generations of American designers with collections that encompassed the principles of comfort, ease and practical lifestyle dressing. During the post-war years, New York became an established fashion capital on its own terms, exporting American design around the world and hosting one of the most prestigious fashion week events on the fashion calendar.

Italy has a long tradition of textile production and regional dressing and Italian style has influenced wider European fashion since the Renaissance. Italy's emergence as a world centre for fashion is based on the solid foundations of skilled labour practices and traditions of fine craftsmanship, as well as the historic production of textiles. As with so much of Italy's history, regional differences evolved and developed across the dominant centres of Florence, Rome and Milan. Italy's post-war reconstruction effort was characterized by sustained investment and growth aligned to private family businesses and a vertically integrated industry, capable of producing fine textiles and the manufacture of quality clothing and accessories. A 'Made in Italy' label adds kudos to a design and confirms Italy's distinctive position as a centre of excellence. Milan is one of the four major fashion capitals alongside Paris, London and New York.

01

GLOBAL FASHION CAPITALS

By the 1980s, Paris, Milan, London and New York were all recognized as established fashion capitals, each distinctive in their own way and all visited by international buyers and press. While these national capitals promoted their own domestic design talent, what has made them even more distinctive is their representation of global design. Some elements of the French press may have scoffed at the arrival of the new wave of Japanese designers during the early 1980s, most notably Rei Kawakubo for Commes des Garçons and Yohji Yamamoto. These designers, in addition to a number of Belgian designers including Dries Van Noten and Dirk Bikkembergs, have not only rejuvenated fashion but also heralded a new era of global fashion design with Paris, Milan, New York and London all hosting internationally diverse fashion events.

The past two decades have also witnessed the emergence of over 30 fashion week events spanning six continents. Fashion weeks now take place in cities from Sao Paulo to Auckland and Moscow to Johannesburg. The ambition for most countries is to promote their local designers and manufacturers while seeking national recognition in a crowded globalized marketplace. The cultural and commercial value of fashion design is regulated by an increasing number of national bodies. Additional trade fairs and expo events have added to the fashion calendar. China is worthy of a special mention thanks to its exponential economic growth as an industrial nation, coupled with its ambition to establish Shanghai as a pre-eminent fashion capital alongside Paris, Milan, London and New York. The Shanghai Expo in 2010 and the city's annual International Fashion Culture Festival have announced China's arrival as a major player in the fashion industry.

Creativity is thinking new things. Innovation is doing new things. **THEODORE LEVITT**

01

02

01—03 _ GLOBAL FASHION WEEKS
Fashion week events in Zagreb, Malaysia and Moscow. Acquiring an international reputation for fashion is an aspiration for many countries to enhance national identity.

03

Global culture

TRICKLE-DOWN EFFECT

TRICKLE-UP EFFECT

Trends are a recurrent feature of fashion design. Trend cycles are based on significant or prevailing indicators that directly or indirectly help to shape and define seasonal looks (which, from a commercial perspective, constitute what may be considered as fashion). Conventional fashion marketing theory accommodates two opposing influences on the fashion trend cycle: the trickle-down effect and the trickle-up or bubble-up effect.

This theoretical model asserts that fashion 'trickles down' from groups that occupy a higher socio-economic status to groups with a lower socio-economic status. Historically this model fits a system where clothing and dress styles primarily denoted status and rank. The inception and rise of haute couture during the nineteenth and early twentieth centuries wholly endorsed this model while asserting a hierarchical system of fashion.

The trickle-up effect works in opposition to trickle-down. In this model, trends are created at a lower level such as a popular street style that crosses over into the mainstream or trickles up to designer level. Alternatively, this theoretical model accommodates a trickle-up effect that might start from a popular music genre or sports influence to a counter-culture group such as punk or hip-hop.

Today most fashion marketers accommodate the existence of both effects. When applied to the context of post-modernism, fashion design continually refreshes itself through a series of diverse and sometimes opposing influences. These are further enabled through expanding media and communication channels, including fashion shows. Broader themes from fast-fashion to eco-fashion have extended fashion design's vocabulary and semiotics in the twenty-first century.

01

01 __ GWEN STEFANI
Gwen Stefani has become a contemporary style icon, launching her own design label L.A.M.B with a flirtatious mix of clothing, accessories and perfume. Flanked by her Harajuku girls, these dancers present a stylized expression of Japanese street fashion.
Credit: PF / Keystone USA / Rex Features

MEDIA COMMUNICATION

'Getting it right' commercially remains crucial to all fashion businesses from design to point-of-sale. This requires a balanced approach to understanding market conditions with a critical appreciation for timing. Timing in fashion holds a special significance and is frequently linked to the cyclical selling seasons. In this regard, the fashion industry is served by a number of professional authorities and organizations that are engaged in the continuous business of trend and forecasting analysis, including colour and textile forecasts, identifying macro trends and summary analysis of the international fashion shows and biannual trade exhibitions.

Contemporary fashion is part of global media and culture. From the early Paris fashion plates of the eighteenth century to the unique marketing capabilities of user-generated social media in the twenty-first century, fashion has always been represented across a full range of media channels. Contemporary fashion media extends far beyond the traditional print-based formats of fashion and style magazines to include websites, blogs, image and video hosting services, social-media communications and the micro-blogging capabilities of Twitter. Each media channel offers its own view of fashion where the distinction between myth and reality is conveniently blurred or conspicuously separated out depending upon the desired impact or effect. In the end, the myths and realities of contemporary fashion co-exist while competing ideologies persuade fashion consumers to be fashionable. Branding contributes to this process by seemingly transferring human values and characteristics onto the fashion brand itself. Celebrities and models have also become 'fashion designers' or 'brands' as they promote their own lines or collections as part of the global fashion design and media industries.

02 — SOKO
Social enterprise fashion label SOKO, based in Kenya, works with local cooperatives and crafts people to produce fashion-driven garments for local and export markets. Most recently SOKO has collaborated with online fashion store ASOS for the launch of ASOS Africa.
Credit: SOKO

02

Q&A
Lee Lapthorne

Name

Lee Lapthorne

Occupation

Designer and founder/director of doll and On|Off

Website

www.leelapthorne.com

Biography

Lee is one of the country's leading fashion and event management experts. His clients include BBC, ITV, P&G, CKOne, SKY, Range Rover and Italian *Vogue*.

As the founder and director of doll and On|Off, Lee has produced, directed and called shows for Gucci, Pam Hogg, Robert Cary-Williams, Preen, Jasper Conran, Nicole Farhi and Gardem during Paris and London Fashion Weeks.

He has produced award-winning commercial productions for the Clothes Show Live, Britain's Next Top Model Live and Westfield.

Lee is also an external examiner for the BA Print course at Central Saint Martins Print and he is a council member for Coolbrands. He has been described by *Design Week* magazine as one of the country's hottest creative talents in its annual list of the 50 most important people in fashion and design today.

Tell us about your agency, doll, and why you founded it.

doll is a creative events agency and consultancy to the fashion industry. It provides integrated event production for fashion shows, product launches, press days, awards, parties and bespoke events.

In early 2000, I was art directing and producing exciting catwalk shows for designers like Emma Cook, Robert Cary-Williams and Preen, at a time when Britannia was still 'cool'. My name was becoming synonymous with producing creative and directional shows. I was conscious that these big shows included a team of creatives and that's how doll was born, in 2003.

The name 'doll' comes from my final MA textiles project, which looked at the way dolls are either cherished for life or are thrown away – a pertinent metaphor for the fashion industry.

What motivated you to set up On|Off?

Designers were always asking me to find new locations and create shows that were unique but always on a shoestring budget! I became close friends with many of them; I was passionate and strived to support them on many levels.

On|Off's first event was in September 2003, and was borne out of my need to create an exciting, distinctive event that supported designers under one roof, which ran parallel to the British Fashion Council's London Fashion Week. The first of its kind, On|Off was revolutionary and forward-thinking, and still is. Our model has since been replicated by other organizations.

On|Off has become a truly international showcase and is the centrepiece of fashion weeks in London, Milan and Paris.

Tell us about some of On|Off's most memorable achievements.

It's been a memorable journey and continues to be a challenge. Four things stand out for me. In 2006, less than two weeks before we were due to open On|Off at the Royal Academy of Arts, a fire destroyed part of the building and we had to move the whole event to the Royal Horticultural Halls. It is testament to the On|Off team that all our designers followed us.

Seeing the industry party hard and sing along with our acts Marc Almond and Soul II Soul in London, and more recently Jessie J at our Paris Fashion Week party, stands out. As do designers' shows that make your hair stand on end such as Gareth Pugh, Pam Hogg and Charlie Le Mindu. We've launched careers for Peter Pilotto, Mark Fast, Yang Du, Osman, Emilio De Le Maria and Hannah Marshall.

But particular highlights were meeting and greeting Anna Wintour at the back door and then HRH The Princess Michael of Kent at the front door of the same show; and, without question, accompanying Isabella Blow around the exhibition for the first time. She always took time with the designers and they loved her.

01 — CHARLIE LE MINDU
Hairdresser and wig designer Charlie Le Mindu presents his catwalk collections as part of the On|Off schedule. This is his AW11 collection, 'Berlin Syndrome.'
Credit: Lee Lapthorne

When you take on a project for a client, how do you balance your vision with your client's expectations?

Flexibility, compromise, clear communication and professionalism are key.

It's important to understand fully the client's business and what they are seeking to achieve. doll is experienced at creating innovative environments that reflect a client's brand. I often produce a focused series of presentations communicating my vision. These presentations are usually packed with references to contemporary art, design, theatre, cinema, music – anything that I feel is relevant. I use PowerPoint, Youtube, photographs/films I've shot, drawings, illustrations, music clips – any way that communicates my ideas. My aim is always to produce a show/event that is an entire audience experience, which is memorable and personalized. I'm passionate about introducing art, designers and experience to my shows. Attention to detail is everything.

What do you love most about your job?

Variety. No two jobs/clients are ever the same and I love the challenge.
Our track record of supporting and delivering design over hype is testament to our professionalism and passion for the survival of our design industry. Also meeting and working with talented creative people is a buzz.

What are your plans for the future?

doll: I'm loving working with brands that want to make a difference, push the boundaries and produce large projects/ events. I would like to work more in the realms of large productions where I direct and work with multimedia.

On|Off: each season I question why and how we continue to grow and develop. I'm always searching for new opportunities, which personally challenge and keep me engaged. As we move forward as an international brand I'd like to work more closely with the other fashion capitals to build a truly global platform. I'm also very interested in e-commerce to support our designers further.

As a successful collaborative platform, On|Off strives to showcase the best of innovative art and design talent. When I meet a talented designer I want to help them succeed.

01—03 _ ON | OFF
On|Off takes place during London Fashion Week and aims to showcase the work of emerging talent. It has supported 170 designers and artists over the years, including designer Pam Hogg, who returned to the catwalks in 2008.
Credit: Lee Lapthorne

01

02

1.0 FASHION IN CONTEXT

03

Discussion questions
Activities
Further reading

DISCUSSION QUESTIONS

ACTIVITIES

DISCUSSION QUESTIONS

1 Evaluate competing definitions of fashion. Discuss these in relation to a variety of social, cultural and political contexts.

2 Discuss why fashion changes over time. Critically evaluate what this tells us about the nature of fashion from a variety of social, psychological, cultural and economic perspectives.

3 Discuss the value and purpose of haute couture in the twenty-first century. Consider its relevance in relation to competing digital technologies and ready-to-wear lines.

ACTIVITIES

1 Identify a contemporary fashion trend. Analyse its evolution and market influence. Looking ahead, prepare a trend board incorporating selected images and artwork based on your individual research and analysis of an emerging design theme.

2 Select a fast-fashion label and an eco-fashion label or brand. Compare and contrast their philosophies and seasonal offers. Consider what they can learn from each other. Create a storyboard for both fashion labels and link this to a potential design theme. Present your boards with a critical justification for both business models.

3 Collect a variety of contemporary fashion advertisements. Evaluate the visual imagery and intended fashion or lifestyle communications of the label or brand. Write a critical essay in response to your selected advertisements by considering the representation or misrepresentation of fashion in relation to a set of chosen socio-cultural contexts.

FURTHER READING

Fashion is architecture.
It is a matter of
proportions. COCO CHANEL

Barnard, M
**Fashion as
Communication**
Routledge, 2002

Barnard, M
Fashion Theory: A Reader
Routledge, 2007

Barthes, R
The Language of Fashion
Berg Publishers, 2006

Breward, C
**The Culture of Fashion:
A New History of
Fashionable Dress
(Studies in Design &
Material Culture)**
Manchester University
Press, 1995

Buxbaum, G
**Icons of Fashion: The
20th Century (Prestel's
Icons)**
Prestel, 2005

Craik, J
Fashion (Key Concepts)
Berg Publishers, 2009

Entwistle, J
**The Fashioned Body:
Fashion Dress and
Modern Social Theory**
Polity Press, 2000

Ewing, E
**History of 20th Century
Fashion**
Batsford Ltd, 2005

Hebdige, D
**Subculture: The Meaning
of Style (New Accents)**
Methuen Publishing Ltd,
1979

Jackson, T & Shaw, M
**The Fashion Handbook
(Media Practice)**
Routledge, 2006

Jones, T
Fashion Now: v. 2 (Big Art)
Taschen GmbH, 2008

Koda, H
**Extreme Beauty: The
Body Transformed
(Metropolitan Museum
of Art)**
Yale University Press, 2004

Lee, S & du Preez, W
**Fashioning the Future:
Tomorrow's Wardrobe**
Thames & Hudson, 2007

Martin, R; Mackrell, A;
Rickey, M & Menkes, S
The Fashion Book
Phaidon Press, 2001

Mendes, V & de la Haye, A
20th Century Fashion
Thames & Hudson, 1999

Svendsen, L
Fashion: A Philosophy
Reaktion Books, 2006

Wilcox, C
Radical Fashion
V&A Publications, 2003

London Fashion Week
**www.londonfashionweek.
co.uk**

Milan Fashion Week
www.cameramoda.it

New York Fashion Week
**www.mbfashionweek.
com**

Paris Fashion Week
www.modeaparis.com

Lagerfeld Confidential
DVD, 2007

**Marc Jacobs & Louis
Vuitton**
DVD, 2008

2.0 THE FASHION FIGURE

OBJECTIVES

To identify appropriate media for fashion drawing

To understand the fashion figure with reference to stylized proportions

To consider line quality, gestures and poses in fashion drawings and visual compositions

To evaluate figurative drawing techniques for men and women

To recognize a variety of fashion drawing formats

To consider digital graphics software applications appropriate to fashion drawing

01 — FASHION DRAWING
Pencil illustration inspired by the work of photographer Richard Bush for *Numero* magazine.
Credit: Mengjie Di

01

Mengste Do Jung 10. 2010

Drawing media for fashion

PAPER

Drawing media for fashion design encompasses a variety of hand-drawing materials and computer-aided design (CAD) software, which can be used independently of each other or in combination. The process of drawing is best developed and improved with regular practice and will ultimately depend upon the designer's vision and clarity of purpose.

Selecting appropriate drawing media is an important consideration. The first thing to consider is the type of paper: the drawing media should be appropriate for the paper quality. A fundamental starting point is to identify and evaluate the right and wrong side of the paper as well as its texture and weight. Specific drawing papers have been developed by commercial art suppliers so there is plenty of choice. The main paper qualities include the following:

NEWSPRINT

This is a lightweight, inexpensive paper that is particularly suitable for charcoal and chalk pastel drawings. Available in a variety of sizes, newsprint can be used for fashion life-drawings as well as for quick sketches. It is usually made from recycled paper in an off-white cast.

TRACING PAPER

Tracing paper is a transparent paper with a smooth surface that is suitable for pencils or pens. This type of paper is particularly useful for creating overlays and tracing over a fashion sketch or drawing for further use or to make corrections. It is generally used for working drawings rather than finished artwork.

MULTIMEDIA VELLUM PAPER

This is a good, general-purpose white paper that can be used with a variety of hand-drawing media including pencils, marker pens and oil-based pastels. This versatile paper can be used for portfolio artwork.

MARKER PAPER

A semi-opaque paper that has been specifically produced to work with a variety of marker pens, marker paper is bleed-proof, which makes it an effective choice for producing colour artworks and working drafts.

LAYOUT PAPER

A lightweight, semi-opaque white paper that is popular for producing line-up sheets or working layouts. It is a good alternative to tracing paper for producing overlays but can also be used for presenting working drawings in a variety of media including pencil and inks.

BRISTOL PAPER

Also referred to as Bristol board, this paper has a high-quality opaque finish and can be used for final artwork presentations. Bristol paper is suitable for pencils, technical pens, pen-and-ink and brush work. Most types are finished on both sides, which makes it suitable for media such as chalk and charcoal.

01 — WORK SPACE
Setting up a suitable workspace is an important starting point when preparing to draw by hand or work with a computer.
Credit: Mengjie Di

01

HAND-DRAWING MEDIA

In addition to choosing the most suitable paper, fashion designers also have a wide choice of hand-drawing media at their disposal. Here are the main art supplies that are most commonly used:

PENCILS

Pencils are one of the most useful and versatile drawing media for fashion designers. They are available across a wide range of grades from 9H to the softest 9B; most fashion designers work with carbon graphite pencils between 2H and 2B. The softer B grades are particularly suitable for producing quick fashion sketches and respond well to pressure and speed variations, which can enable expressive line qualities.

Colour pencils provide a useful addition to a fashion designer's art supplies. Composed of pigment and clay, colour pencils can be used on their own or mixed with other media including marker pens and watercolour washes. Colour pencils can be used to apply specific details and fabric renderings to illustrations and compositions.

MARKER PENS

The introduction of felt-tip marker pens in the 1960s transformed fashion drawing and enabled the move towards more stylized illustration styles for fashion design. They can be used to produce an instant wash across a wide range of colours. Available in a wide variety of nibs, felt-tips are well suited to more vigorous, expressive drawings with a sketch-like quality.

TECHNICAL PENS

Technical pens have precision nibs and are mostly used by fashion designers to produce clean linear drawings and hand-drawn flats where a constant line is required. They provide a viable choice when compared to computer vector graphics, such as Adobe Illustrator, and can also be combined with other drawing media.

CHARCOAL

Charcoal is a useful medium for figurative life drawing and works well on newsprint and textured papers. Available as a charcoal stick or in pencil form, charcoal is noted for its bold lines and tonal rendering properties. Working with charcoal is an expressive experience where precision should not be the primary objective.

PASTELS

Oil pastels are a good option for fashion designers who want to produce a vibrant colour illustration. Their waxy consistency produces an oily appearance, which can be dissolved and smudged by adding turpentine if a softer colour or hue is required. They can also be combined with other media such as chinagraph pencil or gouache as part of an illustration.

Chalk pastels offer a drier, powdery consistency when compared with oil pastels. Made from a combination of limestone and colour pigment, they offer a soft tone colour palette that most people associate with the word pastel. Chalk pastels work well on newsprint paper and can be smudged and blended to provide tonal qualities for life drawing or fashion illustrations.

CHINAGRAPH PENCILS

Also known as China markers, chinagraph pencils are a hard wax pencil rather like a crayon, with an outer wrap at the tip that can be pulled away as it is used. These pencils work well as an alternative to softer charcoals for fashion life drawing; they produce bold lines rather than fine detailing and can be used to add or enhance line quality.

PEN AND INK

This has largely been replaced by marker pens for fashion design artwork today, yet this medium offers a distinctive look that is relevant to fashion illustration. Inks can be applied with a nibbed pen or a brush to produce a range of wash effects. Sable brushes are among the best quality and available in a range of sizes. India ink is a popular choice among fashion designers and illustrators; many fashion illustrators still choose to work with it despite advances with computer software that can replicate the characteristics of pen and ink. As with most hand-drawing processes, working with pen and ink is a labour of love that is capable of producing some sensitive artwork.

GOUACHE

Gouache is an opaque watercolour paint that was developed for designers rather than artists; it produces a flat, even colour when applied correctly. It was a popular medium among fashion designers between the 1930s and 1950s and is used today for illustration work where a brush rather than the vigour and strokes of a marker pen would be more suited to the final artwork.

WATERCOLOUR

Watercolour is effective for creating wash effects; it can be used on its own or combined with pen or linear drawings but should not be overworked or layered into an opaque colour. Watercolour is good for rendering lightweight, sheer fabrics and soft prints and is generally used for womenswear drawings.

As a fashion designer, I was always aware that I was not an artist, because I was creating something that was made to be sold, marketed, used, and ultimately discarded. **TOM FORD**

01 — THE DRAWING PROCESS
Drawing is a process that requires keen observation and hand-to-eye coordination. Over time and with developing confidence, fashion students can enhance their appreciation of drawing and extend their practical and compositional skills.
Credit: Alick Cotterill

01

Understanding the fashion figure

The fashion figure for a designer represents an evolving ideal of the human form; it is used to effectively present and communicate a specific design idea or a desired style. The basis of the fashion figure is called a template or a croquis , on which clothing styles can be drawn and designed. Developing a template is a useful exercise for fashion students and designers alike as it can facilitate the sketching and design process. A successful fashion drawing should look effortless rather than overworked. This is not easy to achieve and can often present a challenge to many fashion design students; however, with a critical eye, practice and an understanding of figurative drawing for fashion design, a personal drawing style can be developed and refined.

Fashion design drawing is characterized by stylization, selective emphasis and exaggerated proportions; it is used to interpret and convey aesthetic information about a design. Because it is more concerned with presenting an ideal form rather than an actual representation of the human body, fashion drawing is not limited by realism; human proportions may be selectively interpreted to give emphasis to some aspects of the design. In this context we may refer to figurative drawing in fashion rather than figure drawing. Although life drawing is relevant to fashion design students, the model should be understood as a point of reference from which to adapt and interpret line and movement. The eye must be trained to critically select the required information from observing a life model. Ultimately, what you draw will depend upon what you are looking for and how you interpret what you see. The first thing to look for when studying a standing fashion figure is balance and weight distribution, which affects the way in which the fashion figure is able to stand or support itself. A symmetrical standing figure is useful for evaluating fashion proportions but is generally less applicable to the development of stylized fashion drawings where asymmetry and gestures enable more expressive poses.

Croquis
A French word that means 'sketch'. In fashion, the term refers to a quick sketch of a figure with a loose drawing of the clothes that are being designed.

01 — LIFE DRAWING
Drawing from life is the best way to observe and study the human figure by evaluating it from different angles and positions. Fashion drawing relies on the ability to reference the human figure.
Credit: Alick Cotterill

01

2.0 THE FASHION FIGURE

PROPORTION

THE BALANCE LINE

The fashion figure is measured in heads. For a woman, the fashion proportion may be 9 or 10 heads to the overall height of the standing figure. This represents a fashion proportion that does not exist in real life but which has become an accepted fashion standard.

As a guide, the standing female figure can broadly be divided into three sections of equal, vertical height. The first section is measured from the top of the head to the waist, then the waist to the knee and finally from the knee to the toes. The lowest section of the standing figure is the most flexibly proportioned and can be adapted to a 9- or 10-heads scale.

The standing female fashion figure has three main horizontal intersections: the shoulder-line, the waist and the hips. These three intersections all respond to weight transference and are critical to convincingly representing movement through the body, depending upon whether the figure is transferring bodyweight from one leg to the other.

For a fashion figure to 'stand' on a page it is essential to understand the balance line. This is an imaginary straight line that drops vertically from the base of the neck to the floor. When the standing figure is symmetrical the balance line falls evenly between the legs but when the standing figure transfers any weight on to one leg, the foot of the weight-supporting leg must be realigned to touch the balance line. This will require the leg of the standing figure to be drawn with a pronounced but gentle curve from the hip to the end of the foot. The angle of the hips should be adjusted to accommodate the transference of weight, resulting in movement through the torso up to the shoulder line. The placement of the arms and the non-supporting leg may be adjusted to suit the intended pose or convey a particular gesture.

Line quality is an important attribute of an effective fashion design drawing. It refers to the thickness or fineness of a line, as well as its speed and texture; a line that is drawn slowly will have different properties to a line that is drawn with speed or vigour. Understanding line quality can greatly enhance a fashion drawing by adding personality and sensitivity to an artwork. It can also give emphasis to an aspect of the drawing such as garment detail, rendering the texture of a fabric or communicating a specific silhouette or fit. The most effective fashion drawings and illustrations are often the result of a combination of lines; however, in fashion design it is better to draw one convincing line rather than three or four. The best fashion drawings present essential information in the most direct way and do not rely on superfluous details or unnecessary shading.

01 — FASHION FIGURES
Working with marker pens offers quick results and a wide choice of colours.
Credit: Hanyuan Guo

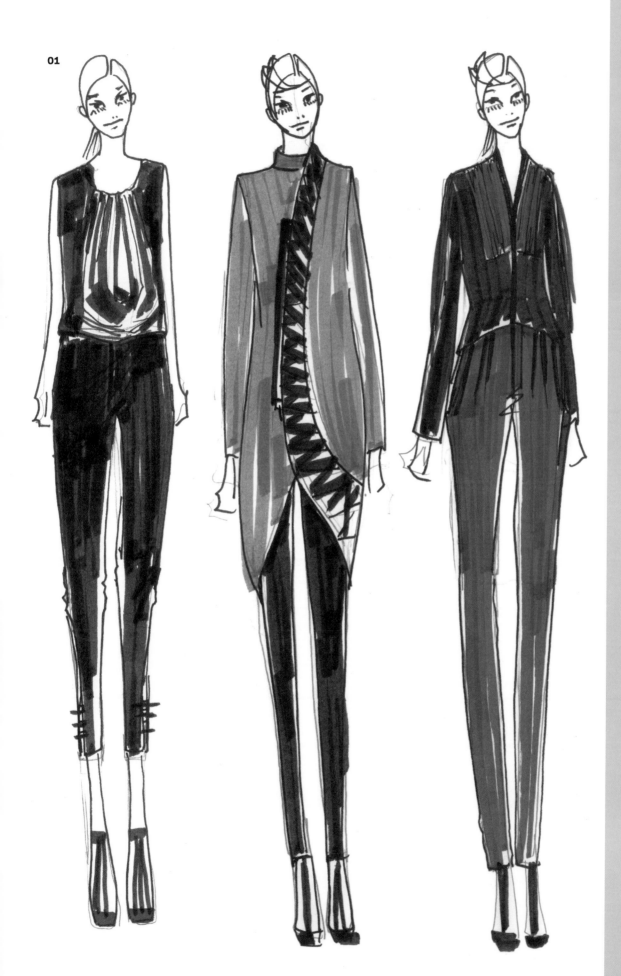

01

DEVELOPING POSES AND GESTURES

Poses are an integral component of figurative fashion drawings. They can directly communicate or imply a mood or an attitude that in turn can help to sell a design or make it recognizable. When considering how to select a suitable pose a good starting point is to collect and analyse a variety of poses from fashion and style photoshoots. You will probably notice that the fashion models have been cast in a variety of poses. Each pose will have been considered by the photographer in relation to the desired mood or attitude to be communicated. In this way it is also important to plan fashion drawings and illustrations by considering each pose as an important part of a figurative drawing.

The fashion figure should appear to be standing on the page with the supporting leg drawn in relation to the balance line. Then the non-supporting leg and arms can be arranged to contribute to the pose or convey a gesture. Tracing over a photograph is a useful starting point and offers an alternative to producing observational drawings. The photograph will serve as a guide for producing preliminary figurative sketches; however, it will be necessary to make adjustments to the 9- or 10-heads vertical proportion. The preliminary sketch can then be traced over as many times as required to develop a more refined and proportioned line drawing.

01 — **LINEAR DRAWING**
Drawing the fashion figure requires an understanding of how to interpret what you see and adapt it to an ideal standard. As a rule, use as few lines as possible to convey as much information as you need to represent.
Credit: HollyMae Gooch

01

FASHION HEADS, FACES AND HAIR

Fashion faces and hairstyles reflect popular trends and cultural preferences. They can also communicate age, mood, ethnicity and individual personality, just as in real life. For the purposes of fashion design the accepted rules are that faces should not be overworked or detract from the design of the clothing. The most significant facial features to consider are the eyes and the lips. Noses and ears are not emphasized.

When drawing a face the overall shape of the head is important: for women, an oval-shaped head is the most appropriate, with the eyes positioned halfway down and set wide apart. As in real life, eyes have the capacity to connect directly with the viewer and should be drawn with due consideration. The upper eyelids and eyelashes can be emphasized with a thick or smudged line. The nose is discreetly positioned midway between the eyes and the chin. A single shadow-effect line down one side of the nose is usually enough with the nostrils indicated by shaded lines or dots. The mouth is positioned just below the nostrils and can be emphasized with a pronounced top lip in a splayed 'M' shape and a well-rounded lower lip. Jaw lines are not be emphasized on women and should be gently rounded to a blunt point; necks are elongated and always slim.

Hairstyles should reflect contemporary taste and style. While the hair should not be overworked, a lack of attention to a hairstyle can diminish a figurative drawing or fashion illustration. Hair may be shaded in combination with a variety of lines to convey an appropriate style.

02 — BUILDING UP FACES
Drawing heads and faces involves a combination of studying the proportions of the face and building up the features, including hair that might be emphasized.
Credit: HollyMae Gooch

02

HANDS, ARMS, LEGS AND FEET

The arms, legs, hands and feet of a fashion figure all contribute to the overall balance and movement of a figurative drawing. Although they may not always be visible, the placement of a model's limbs should be considered in relation to the design of the clothing and footwear. It is generally good practice to draw all limbs and feet with as few lines as possible by applying longer, more continuous lines and avoiding short 'scratch' lines.

Muscle tone is not emphasized for women. Instead, arms and legs should be drawn using a series of long, gently curving lines. Legs should be drawn with consideration of the thigh, knee and calf, which are all interconnected but distinct from each other. Curvature is emphasized through the outer leg from the hip position while the knee and foot should be drawn more discreetly, with a few curved lines including a narrow but defined ankle. While feet will often be dressed with a shoe, for open-toe sandals draw a long, narrow foot with angled toes.

Hands can offer an expressive element to a successful figurative fashion drawing and, while they are not emphasized for women, they should be considered. A common mistake is to draw a hand like a club or mitten. The wrist will enable the position of the hand to be defined with a gently curved palm, long narrow fingers and a narrow thumb.

01 _ HANDS
A study of hands.
Credit: HollyMae Gooch

02 _ FEET
A study of feet.
Credit: HollyMae Gooch

01

02

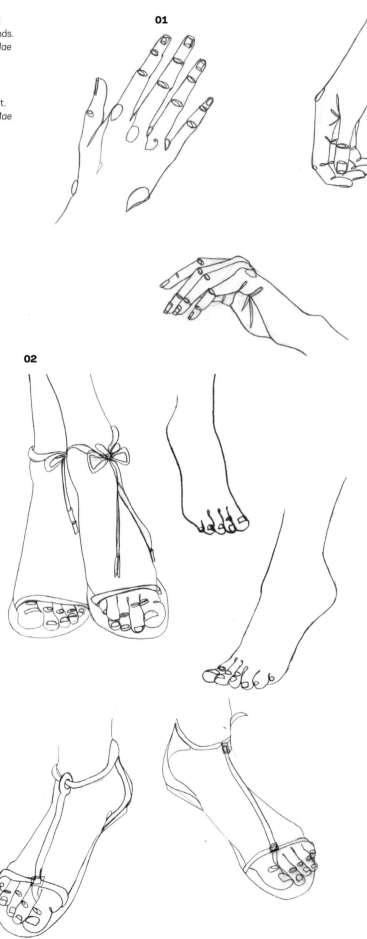

SILHOUETTES

In the context of figurative drawing, fashion silhouettes refer to the overall outline shape of the clothed fashion figure. Some silhouettes follow or accentuate the human form, while others obscure or deny it through dramatic manifestations of volume and structure. Over time, fashion silhouettes have provided a visual record of the main evolutionary changes in fashion such as the introduction of the high-waisted empire-line dress during the early nineteenth century or the square padded shoulders that graced many of the Paris fashion shows during the 1980s. From a fashion design perspective silhouettes are the result of design decisions relating to cut, fit and volume. Individual garments such as a skirt or pants can have a defined impact on the overall silhouette of a figure.

When drawing an individual garment or a collection line-up, the cut and drape of all the garments will produce a series of shapes that should be reviewed and evaluated for their consistency and aesthetic appeal. A fashion silhouette should be contemporary and relevant but should also reflect an understanding of the fashion figure from a three-dimensional perspective. Fashion illustration enables more artistic expression than a design sketch or line drawing. This has resulted in some illustrators producing artworks with a bold, dramatic look or a romantic appearance. However, the most accomplished illustrators have an understanding of fabric and the construction process, using both elements to produce a discernible line or internal movement that contributes to the overall silhouette. Variations in line quality can be used to emphasize and enhance the silhouette of a figurative drawing, while directing the viewer's eye to the main focus of a design.

03 — SILHOUETTES
Pen-and-ink drawing of male and female figures.
Credit: Mengjie Di

03

THE MALE FASHION FIGURE

The male fashion figure is also drawn with a level of personal interpretation and selective emphasis; however, as a guide men's proportions are less exaggerated than for women.

Aside from the obvious anatomical differences, the main difference to consider when drawing the male fashion figure is muscle tone. This is much more pronounced in men and determines some of the vertical proportions. Although the standing male figure can also be 9 heads, or even 10, it does not gain extra length through the lower legs but through the torso, which is emphasized with a broad chest. A youthful male fashion figure should convey a healthy, active look. If a man and woman are standing next to each other, make sure that the man is the same height or slightly taller than the woman.

The head of a man is less oval than for a woman. Instead the jaw line is squared off and a chin dimple can be added. Lips are not emphasized and may be drawn using straight, narrow lines. Eyebrows may be emphasized with a straight nose. Realistic facial and clothing details are generally more typical of menswear illustrations. Facial hair may be added if this supports the intended look but full beards are less applicable. The neck is drawn thicker than for a woman; it is not as elongated. The main emphasis for a man is the chest and shoulder area. The shoulders are drawn much wider and the arms have additional mass and muscle tone. The waist position is less defined and is drawn in a lower position so that the upper chest and body are more prominent. Stomach muscles can be included if this is appropriate, while the hips are much less pronounced and curved than for a woman and are drawn almost vertically to the thigh of the leg.

01 — MALE POSE
Pen-and-ink drawing of seated male figure wearing a hat.
Credit: Mengjie Di

02 — MALE FIGURE
The male fashion figure is generally less exaggerated than for women and drawn with more emphasis on individual muscle tone.
Credit: HollyMae Gooch

01

Less is more.

LUDWIG MIES VAN DER ROHE

02

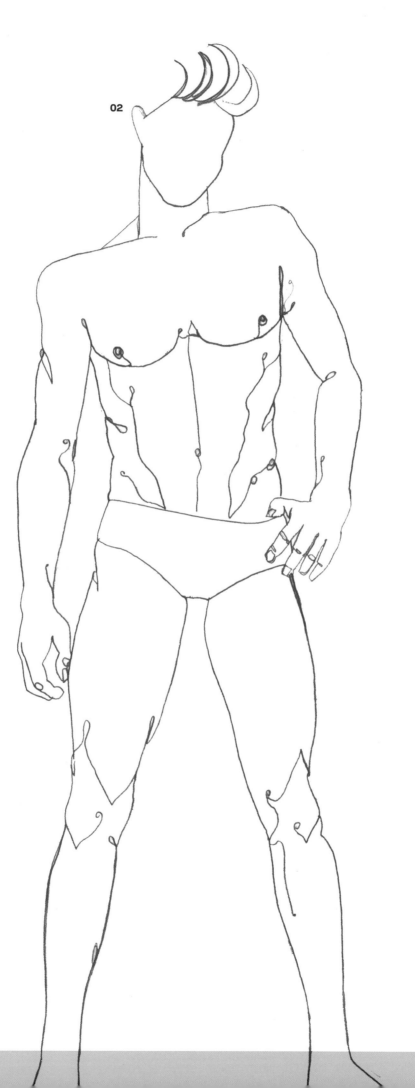

DRAWING MEN

To convincingly draw a man it is essential that the hips are noticeably narrower than the chest and upper shoulders, which should always be the broadest part of the male figure. Men's legs are drawn with muscle tone; thicker and a little shorter than for a woman, while the kneecap and feet can be more pronounced. A man's feet may be drawn larger and in a more angular style; calves and ankles are also defined. The supporting leg isn't drawn with the same amount of curve, since a man's pelvis is less pronounced. The hands can also be more pronounced, with realistically proportioned fingers and a thicker wrist.

When drawing from life, it is essential to study the pose before you begin to draw. Remember there is no substitute for analysing the structural elements of each pose. The rules of the balance line also apply to drawing the standing male figure; however, male poses and gestures are more subtle than for women. It is useful to collect tearsheets of male models or athletes from style and fitness magazines. Referring to photographs will help you establish the basis for producing credible poses if you are not life drawing. The type of pose should also reflect the character of the clothing: so an athletic pose, for example, might not be appropriate when drawing a tailored suit or formal outfit.

01

Yuan Shijing

01 — MENSWEAR ILLUSTRATION
It is useful to collect and analyse tearsheets of male models to establish a range of credible poses.
Credit: Shijing Tuan

02 — HANDS
A study of male hands, which are thicker and more pronounced than women's.
Credit: HollyMae Gooch

02

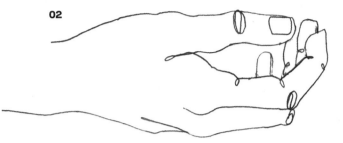

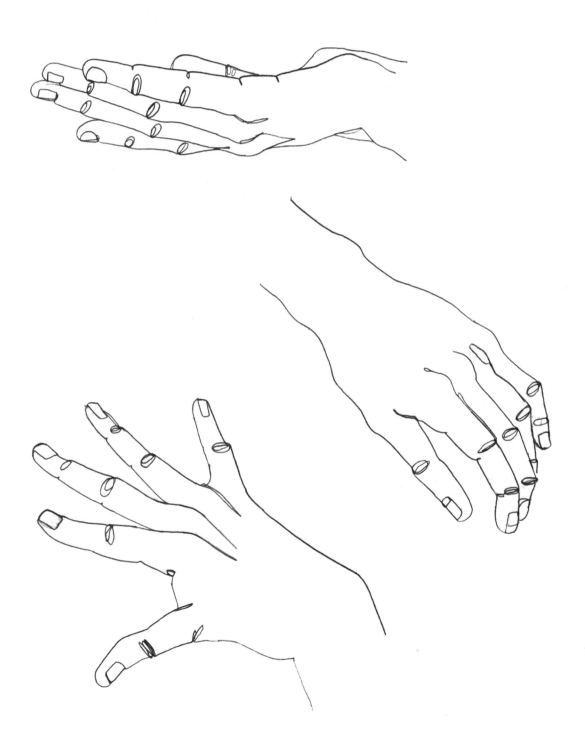

Technical drawings

PRODUCING SPECIFICATION SHEETS AND FLATS

Technical drawings include fashion 'flats' and specification drawings. Both are relevant to the fashion industry and each serves a distinct purpose. A fashion flat refers to a linear drawing of a garment or series of garments, which are drawn as if they were laid down flat and viewed from above. They are used to provide technical information about a design such as the essential shape and cut of a garment and can be drawn in conjunction with a sketch or figurative drawing to clarify a design or enhance a presentation.

A specification drawing or 'spec' is a detailed technical line drawing of a single garment that is drawn for a specification or production sheet. Its sole purpose is to clarify and explain all technical aspects of a design for manufacturing including sizing and measurements. A spec is not enhanced for its artistic or presentation value since this is not its function. Instead a spec sheet will include additional technical information about manufacturing, assembly processes and trimmings.

The ability to produce a technical drawing is an important requirement for a designer in the ready-to-wear fashion industry. Most fashion students will be familiar with spec sheets and flats, but are more likely to produce flats for their portfolios. Despite their name, fashion flats should be drawn with full consideration of the garment, including front and back views. Drawing fashion flats differs in one significant way to figurative drawing. Fashion flats are drawn to a realistically proportioned human figure, such as an 8-heads height. In this way, flats demonstrate a realistic understanding of a garment and present clear visual information about the line and cut of each design.

While fashion flats should always be drawn with clarity, different line thicknesses can be applied. For example, topstitching may need a finer line than a seam line or the outline shape of a pocket (there are a variety of technical pens to assist with this process). In this way, each component of the drawing will be distinct and clear. Fashion flats may be symmetrical but can also be drawn asymmetrically, with a sleeve folded over on one side to reveal a button detail, for example. This helps the flat appear less static and rigid in appearance, reflecting the soft characteristics of most fabrics. You should not have to add any shading to a flat to communicate the design, since all essential information can be drawn with lines. When drawing a fashion flat it can be useful to work to a larger scale before reducing it to the required size. This will make the drawing appear detailed as well as being easier to draw. As a rule, flats should be drawn with as few lines as possible. All details such as seams, pleats, gathers, tucks and folds should be clear and understandable; lines can be drawn to indicate depth, volume or fullness. When working to a presentation format it is good practice to draw all your flats to the same body scale so that a skirt will look in proportion to a jacket, for example.

01

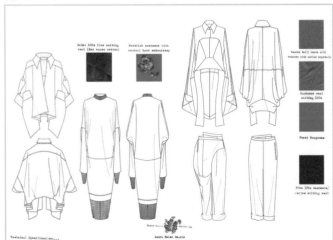
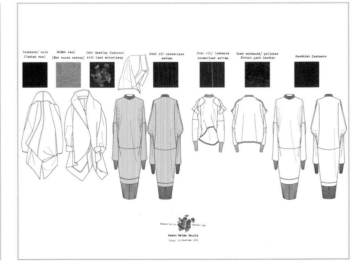

While flats can be drawn alongside a stylized fashion figure they can also be presented individually or as part of a range plan. In this way, a designer can quickly evaluate the number of skirts and pants in a collection in relation to the number of tops, for example. Flats also provide a visual indication to the silhouettes or key looks within a collection.

Vector graphics software has been developed to draw flats and specs with precision and with the addition of presentation enhancement features. However, drawing flats by hand is still a useful skill for fashion designers.

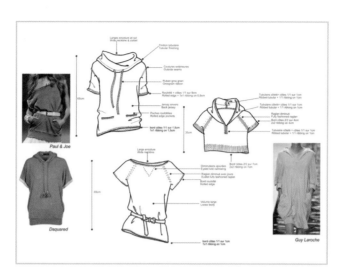

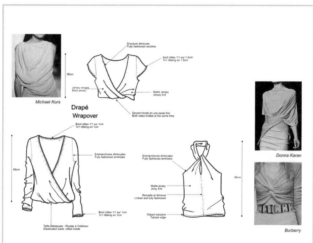

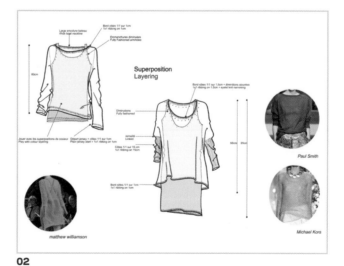

02

01 — TECHNICAL DRAWINGS
Technical drawings with corresponding fabric scans.
Credit: Laura Helen Searle

02 — DRAWINGS AND BOARDS
Fashion flats used to analyse key looks and garment details.
Credit: Catherine Corcier

Fashion illustration

EVOLUTION OF FASHION ILLUSTRATION

ILLUSTRATION TECHNIQUES

Fashion illustration occupies a special place in the visual communication of fashion. Its primary purpose is to visually engage with the viewer. Over time, fashion illustration has become a cultural and artistic barometer of style and taste through the decades.

What passes for a fashion illustration today has evolved through the years, partly as a result of shifts and trends in society as well as through advances in computer technology and wider artistic and aesthetic cultural influences. In the same way that fashion design reflects contemporary values and technologies, fashion illustration remains an evolving practice with artistic and commercial applications. Historically, fashion illustrations were featured in most fashion magazines until photography took over in the 1960s and 70s. The stylized characteristics of fashion illustration were later recognized and revived by some notable fashion magazines and commercial businesses in Europe and the United States. In reality, while fashion illustration and fashion photography are distinct media formats, the development of digital graphics software has boosted the artistic appeal of fashion illustration and extended its commercial reach.

A hand-rendered fashion illustration has the capacity to present an image of the fashion figure that transcends what is real; it communicates what we might imagine or hope for. A fashion illustration should not only communicate visual information about a design but also express a mood or emotion: this remains one of the most important attributes of an effective illustration. Most of the great fashion illustrators, past and present, have understood this principle and worked with life models to enable a full range of expression in their work, such as Antonio Lopez in the 1970s as well as contemporary illustrators such as David Downton. It is interesting to note that many fashion illustrators are not usually trained designers. This is not a handicap but rather a release, which allows them to capture the essence and spirit of a design or outfit without being distracted by too many details or constraints.

Designers who approach fashion illustration do so with a training and a critical eye that compels them to communicate detailed information such as seam lines and individual pleats. Of course, this has its place in a designer's portfolio and can produce a valid form of figurative illustration. However, if a design is clearly communicated through a fashion flat or an equivalent line drawing, then some of the details of a design can be relaxed in an illustration to focus on communicating the spirit or attitude of an outfit. Many of the techniques previously discussed in relation to figurative drawing can be readily applied to fashion illustration and combined with a level of personal expression.

There is a rich variety in media choices for fashion illustration. Hand-drawing processes may be used on their own or in combination with CAD software. For a fashion design student or established practitioner an accomplished fashion illustration adds creative content to a design portfolio and is a good indication of the designer's colour and compositional skills.

**01 — FASHION
ILLUSTRATION**
Pen-and-ink illustration
inspired by the work
of designer Alexander
McQueen.
Credit: Mengjie Di

01

COMPOSITION AND LAYOUT

Drawing a fashion figure is one aspect of fashion illustration. Planning the overall layout and balance of the composition is an important factor in effectively communicating the overall look or message of the artwork. In composition the fashion figure represents the positive image. The surrounding space is referred to as the negative space. Both elements should be carefully considered when a fashion figure is placed on a page so that the eye focuses on the main points of interest without competing with an overworked background. Unplanned colours and superfluous lines can detract from, rather than complement a fashion illustration, so less is more. Some of the most effective fashion illustrations allow the viewer to fill in details with the mind's eye.

An effective composition captures the attention and interest of a viewer while directing the eye to the intended focus of the artwork; it should allow the eye to flow logically over the supporting elements of the image without creating monotony or confusion. The selection and use of colour is largely intuitive and a matter of personal taste. A well-planned fashion illustration will have an alluring appeal that will draw in the viewer and enhance the overall figure.

01 — FASHION ILLUSTRATION
Illustration inspired by the work of designer Angel Sanchez.
Credit: Mengjie Di

02 — FASHION ILLUSTRATION
One of the most important attributes of an effective composition is its ability to convey a mood or emotion.
Credit: Daria Lipatova

01

02

True creativity
often starts
where language
ends. **ARTHUR KOESTLER**

CAD for fashion

Computer-aided design, also known as CAD, has extended the media choices for fashion designers thanks to a wide range of vector and bitmap graphics programs. Some are generic, while others have been specifically developed for the fashion industry.

Most fashion students today are introduced to graphics programs and a variety of digital tools that can facilitate the development and formulation of imagery. Foremost among these are scanners that enable a hand-drawn sketch or photograph to be scanned and saved as a digital image file. Digital cameras have also become a useful tool for fashion designers to record and collect original images that can be downloaded and saved, retouched or resized for later use in a digital artwork or presentation.

Graphics tablets and pens offer more specific tools that fashion designers can use to create digital freehand drawings. As with all hand-drawing processes, freehand drawing requires practice while its capabilities are ultimately dependent upon the vector graphics software being used.

01 — CAD FLATS
Computer-enhanced illustration with corresponding flats.
Credit: Kun Yang

01

**02 __ CAD
ILLUSTRATIONS**
Computer-enhanced
fashion illustrations.
Credit: Shijing Tuan

02

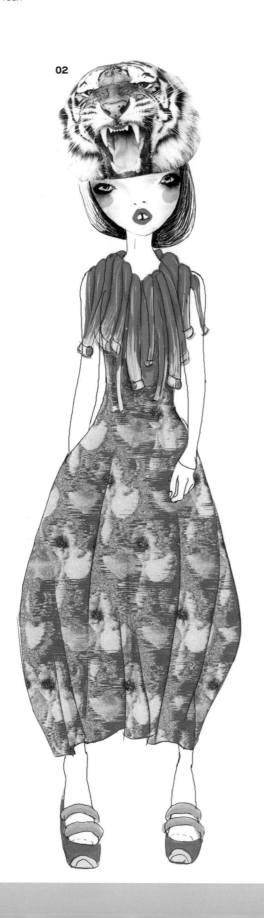

BITMAP IMAGERY

Bitmap image manipulation software, such as Adobe Photoshop, can be applied to the formulation of fashion artwork. The bitmap software is made up of pixels. These are the building blocks of bitmap images and determine the resolution of the image, which can be resized and edited. The menu bars include image correction, retouching tools and digital painting functions. One of the main attributes of digital graphics software, including Photoshop, is the ability to edit and make corrections to scanned images or collected image files. Hand-drawn images can also be scanned and imported using layers palettes to clone, edit or refine a presentation, as well as remove flaws or errors. Photoshop is well suited to the production of mixed media images, which are frequently used in fashion presentations.

VECTOR GRAPHICS

Adobe Illustrator is a widely used vector-based graphics software that offers a variety of digital media options, including the ability to import and combine scanned bitmap images, text and vector graphics to create a versatile media package. Vector graphics can be scaled up or down without losing resolution as they are made up of segments (lines) not pixels. This makes Illustrator ideally suited to a variety of drawing and rendering processes. As well as its pen and pencil tools it has a tracing tool that enables a freehand sketch or drawing to be traced over and saved for use through a series of working layers. Colour fills and stroke options can be used to simulate a wide variety of hand-drawing styles and brush strokes. In addition, there are digital colour libraries such as Pantone fashion colours and a function that enables original scanned fabrics to be imported and embedded into artworks.

FASHION SOFTWARE

There are a number of specialist IT providers that have developed a range of dedicated fashion software. Foremost among these are Lectra in France and SnapFashun in the United States.

Lectra offers a Windows-based graphics media package that has been specifically designed and developed to create effective fashion presentations including moodboards, storyboards, fashion flats and illustrations. Lectra's dedicated fashion design software incorporates a range of time- and labour-saving features such as object-based vector drawings and fabric colourways, as well as 'drag and drop' technology that enables users without advanced digital media skills to produce visually engaging presentations. Original fabrics can also be scanned and imported into artworks.

01

01 — LINE-UP DRAWING
CAD-enhanced line-up of capsule collection.
Credit: Laura Helen Searle

SnapFashun is a digital image library that has been designed specifically to serve the needs of the fashion industry. Its extensive image banks include thousands of vector graphic images of menswear, womenswear and childrenswear. SnapFashun also offers an extensive selection of proportioned garment details such as collars, pockets, sleeves, plackets and waistbands that can be used and resized if necessary. Using Adobe Illustrator or Micrografx Designer, the vector images 'snap' into place when used together to create an instant digital drawing or fashion flat. Offering quick results, this dedicated software program is ideal for ready-made silhouettes and garment details.

CAD offers fashion designers a range of extended opportunities to create and refine ideas and working processes that span all areas of fashion design from technical drawings to fashion illustrations. The ability to work with CAD is increasingly expected in the fashion industry.

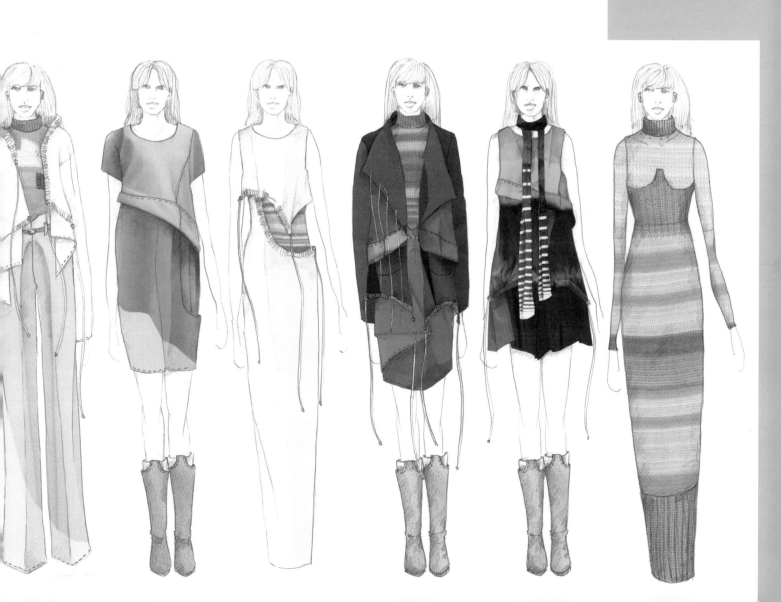

Q&A
Daria Lipatova

Name

Daria Lipatova

Occupation

Fashion and graphic designer

Website

www.deviantart.com

Biography

I have always been interested in visual art, from different illustrations in books and cartoons to classic artworks. I liked to draw from an early age, although when I was little I didn't occupy myself with drawing seriously. Nevertheless, I had good skills in drawing and it allowed me to choose between two creative courses: animation and fashion design. I decided to study fashion design. There was a great course of drawing and painting that became a foundation to form my own style. Now I continue to experiment with different techniques and materials.

How would you describe your fashion drawing style?

I think that the main features of my style are the laconism of silhouettes and dynamic figure setting, based on the styles found in cartoons or comic books.

What type of drawing media do you like to use and why?

I start to draw all my works in pencil. Sometimes I like my sketches in pencil; sometimes I continue to draw them in graphic painting programs. I start with pencil sketches because it gives me a possibility to make changes – erase something, add details and, as opposed to graphic programs, I can draw anywhere and at any time. Drawing in CorelDraw and Photoshop allows me to choose the best colour and texture combinations for every model. Sometimes I use PaintDraw SAI.

How do you develop the poses and gestures in your fashion artwork?

At first I start to draw an abstract silhouette and then fill it with more exact lines. So the silhouette sets poses and sometimes gestures. Also, I try to give naturalness to my characters and reveal their image. At the same time I want my drawings to tell a story about depicted characters.

Do you apply a different style or approach between drawing men and drawing women?

No, I don't have a special approach: I start to draw men's and women's figures equally. In the beginning I draw silhouette lines and then pass on to form. Of course I take into account anatomical features.

From your experience, what elements make up a visually engaging fashion illustration?

I think the main thing is an attractive image; fashion illustration has its own mission – to disclose the image. The high quality of drawing and style are also important. It's very interesting to look at the picture when the illustrator has taken into consideration these things. And to my mind, these things bring illustration closer to art.

Who or what inspires you?

There are so many things that inspire me: cartoons with dynamic and attractive images, works of modern artists, graphics, illustrators, who have new drawing styles and can express the mood of our time, art nouveau, fashion illustration at the beginning of the twentieth century, fashion photography, sketches and designers' illustrations. I was very impressed by the works of Aitor Throup.

01 — FASHION ILLUSTRATION
Abstract figurative illustration.
Credit: Daria Lipatova

01

2.0 THE FASHION FIGURE

01—02 __ FASHION ILLUSTRATIONS
Series of figurative colour illustrations.
Credit: Daria Lipatova

02

Discussion questions
Activities
Further reading

DISCUSSION QUESTIONS

ACTIVITIES

DISCUSSION QUESTIONS

1 Collect some examples of fashion photographs from a variety of magazines and photographic shoots. Discuss how the fashion figure is presented and styled.

2 Identify the work of some fashion illustrators that you admire or find interesting. Discuss their media choices and techniques.

3 Select a variety of drawn and photographic images of faces, hair and make-up. Analyse their differences and appeal with reference to gender, age, mood and ethnicity.

ACTIVITIES

1 Referring to the fashion proportions of the 9- or 10-heads figure and the balance line, draw a standing figure as the basis for developing a personal template or fashion croquis. Start by blocking out the head and dropping the balance line down vertically. Intersect the high hip point between 4.5 and 5 heads down. Draw the hip at an angle and follow the curve of the supporting leg and foot down to the base of the balance line before blocking out the remaining figure with the non-supporting leg, waist and shoulder positions.

2 Experiment with a variety of drawing media, including graphite pencil, charcoal, marker pen and chinagraph pencil to create a series of experimental linear drawings. The fashion subject can either be drawn from direct observation or a suitable photograph. Use as few lines as possible to communicate only essential information and consider the impact of line quality. Remember that an effective fashion drawing can be selective to communicate the essence of the subject without being overworked. Draw from the shoulder and don't be afraid to make mistakes.

3 Collect a variety of garments in different fabrics. Lay each of them out 'flat' and study them. Look at the front and back of each garment noting all details and shaping features. Draw each garment using only lines, without shading. Consider three main lines in your drawing: a silhouette line, which defines the garment's overall shape and proportion; style lines, which define the cut and fit of the garment (both of these should be drawn to realistic proportions); and detail lines, such as topstitching, buttonholes and pockets. Hand-drawn flats can also be scanned and digitally edited or enhanced as vector drawings using graphics software like Adobe Illustrator.

FURTHER READING

The medium is the message. **MARSHALL MCLUHAN**

Blackman, C
**100 Years of Fashion
Illustration**
Laurence King, 2007

Centner, M and Vereker, F
**Adobe Illustrator: A
Fashion Designer's
Handbook**
John Wiley & Sons, 2007

Dawber, M
**Big Book of Fashion
Illustration: A
World Sourcebook
of Contemporary
Illustration**
Batsford, 2007

Downton, D
**Masters of Fashion
Illustration**
Laurence King, 2010

Hopkins, J
**Basics Fashion Design:
Fashion Drawing**
AVA Publishing, 2009

McDowell, C and
Brubach, H
**Drawing Fashion: A
Century of Fashion
Illustration**
Prestel, 2010

Morris, B
Fashion Illustrator
Laurence King, 2010

Packer, W and Hockney, D
Fashion Drawing in Vogue
Thames & Hudson, 2010

Riegelman, N
**9 Heads: A Guide to
Drawing Fashion**
9 Heads Media, 2006

Riegelman, N
**Face Fashion: A Guide to
Drawing the Fashion Face**
9 Heads Media, 2009

Stipelman, S
**Illustrating Fashion 3rd
edition**
Fairchild, 2010

Szkutnicka, B
**Technical Drawing for
Fashion**
Laurence King, 2010

Tallon, K
**Digital Fashion
Illustration**
Batsford, 2008

3.0 COLOUR AND FABRICS

OBJECTIVES

To understand the basic principles of colour theory

To appreciate different colour schemes and the relationship between them

To consider variables between colour characteristics

To consider the role of colour forecasting

To recognize the diversity of textile fibres and fabrics

To critically evaluate diverse fabrics and their potential design applications

---

01 — AMAYA ARZUAGA AW11
Working with colour is a personal and intuitive process that may be used to communicate a fashion look or create a bold statement such as colour blocking.
Credit: Totem / Ugo Camera

Colour theory

SATURATION

HUE

Colour is a fundamental element in fashion design that can evoke an emotional response but is also determined by scientific principles. The associations between colour and light should be clearly understood from the outset: in the absence of light it is not possible to view colour. So it follows that variations in light, whether natural or man-made, directly affect the way in which colour is seen with the human eye. Moreover, the human eye has the capacity to distinguish between a vast range of colour variations; these are generally categorized into the main colours that are visible through a prism, which is known as the colour spectrum.

The colour wheel visually represents the spectrum of electro-magnetic waves of energy from infrared to ultraviolet as if it was joined up in a circle or wheel. The colours on the wheel can be described by three main parameters: saturation, hue and value. Saturation is used to describe the intensity of a colour; it is also referred to as chroma. A highly saturated colour appears bright and is closer to the edge of the colour wheel than an unsaturated colour, which appears duller. A colour that has no saturation or chroma will appear as achromatic or in greyscale.

The second parameter is hue. Hue or spectral colour is represented as an angle and includes the primary colours of red, green and blue and the complementary colours of yellow, cyan and magenta, which are formed by combining two adjacent primary colours (for example, red and blue makes magenta). Hues that are 100% intensity can be described as fully saturated with pigment, but when there is no pigment, a grey of equal value to the pure colour is left. The natural order of hues follows the sequence of a rainbow, running from red to orange to yellow, on to green, blue and purple. Although purple does not appear in a rainbow, it completes the family of hues in the colour wheel.

01

BASIC COLOUR WHEEL

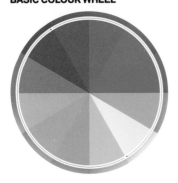

MONOCHROME

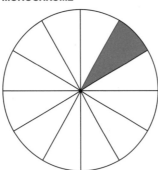

COMP 1

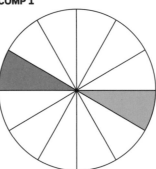

SPLIT 1

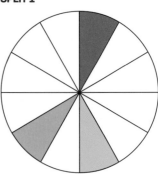

01 — COLOUR WHEELS

Colour wheel theory can be applied to the selection and use of colour combinations in fashion including colours used in prints.

ANALOGOUS

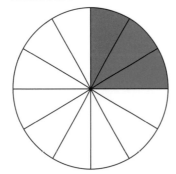

MUTUAL 1

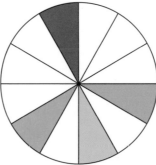

NEAR 1

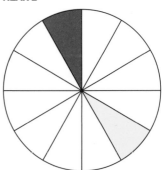

VALUE

SUBTRACTIVE AND ADDITIVE THEORIES

The third parameter is value. This describes the quality by which we may distinguish light colours from dark colours. Specifically, it refers to the luminescent contrast between black and white and is closely aligned to shade and tint. Shade refers to a spectrum colour that is mixed with a proportion of black, while tint represents a colour that is mixed with a proportion of white. Both offer variations of colour value while the resulting shade or tint may be identified as a colour tone. The lightness and darkness of any given hue can be measured according to greyscale.

There are two main colour theories: subtractive and additive. Subtractive or pigment theory is concerned with how white light is absorbed and reflected off coloured surfaces. Since black absorbs most light and white reflects light, coloured pigments absorb light and reflect only the frequency of the pigment colour. Colour is perceived by the human eye when light strikes a surface that contains pigment. All colours other than the pigment are absorbed. This is visually expressed through overlaying the colours used in the subtractive theory, which are cyan, magenta, yellow and black (CMYK), used in printing. Green, violet and orange make up the subtractive secondary colours. When combined in equal amounts, CMYK can be mixed to form black.

The additive theory, also known as light absorption theory, is concerned with radiated and filtered light: white radiates light while black does not. The primary colours in the additive theory are red, green and blue, known collectively as RGB. In the additive theory the primary colours are added together to make white. RGB is the standard colour system used for digital media such as digital cameras, scanners, graphics media and software. RGB colours can be converted to CMYK for commercial printing but are essentially screen-based. Both systems can be used to create colour palettes.

TRI 1

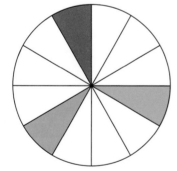

DOUBLE

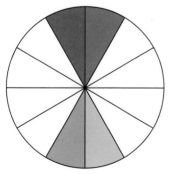

COLOUR SCHEMES

Working with colour requires an understanding of colour schemes. This is particularly relevant to fashion designers. Colour schemes may be understood through a variety of recognized classifications including monochromatic colours, complementary colours, analogous colours, warm colourways, cool colourways, primary and accent colours and achromatic colours.

A monochromatic colour scheme is one in which the same colour hue is used with varying values of shades and tints. Colours with a similar value or chroma generally work well together. In fashion terms, the result will be a fabric or garment that offers variations from one colour hue. In spite of the name, monochromatic colour schemes offer a variety of colour depths through shades and tints but do not include contrasting colours.

A complementary colour scheme combines colours that are positioned as opposites on the colour wheel, such as red and green. The contrast between the two colours is striking; however, the effect sometimes needs to be moderated or restricted within an outfit or garment. A split-complementary colour scheme is a variation in which two adjacent colours are used in addition to the base colour. The resulting colour scheme is also vibrant but the interaction between three colours reduces the visual tension that is characteristic of two complementary colours.

A triadic colour scheme is another variation on the colour wheel where three colours are used in combination based on their evenly spaced position. They can offer a level of vibrancy that should be harmonious so that one colour does not dominate the other two. If this happens, the other colours may take on the appearance of accent colours supporting a dominant colour. If used skilfully, triadic and split-complementary colours can form the basis of effective prints for fashion design.

An analogous colour scheme offers the possibility of mixing and combining colours that are adjacent on the colour wheel. They produce a harmonious look and the effect can be subtle and sophisticated.

01 — JONATHAN SAUNDERS SS11
Fashion designers must consider colours in the context of preparing seasonal collections. Colour palettes for spring/summer collections are likely to be noticeably different to those prepared for the autumn/winter season.
Credit: Catwalking

COLOURWAYS

In fashion design we often talk about warm or cool colourways. This describes colours that make up two halves of the colour wheel. It is a reaction to the perception of a colour's temperature. Reds, oranges and yellows are most commonly associated with warmth, while blues, greens and violets are generally classified as cool colours. Warm and cool colourways can be used to great effect with their own distinct attributes: warm colours appear to be vivid and radiate into the space around them while cool colours appear calm and soothing. Black and white are considered to be neutral and can be combined with warm or cool colours. Fashion designers should be aware of colour attributes and how warm and cool colours can relate to particular fabrics, surface textures and even skin tones in the context of considering seasons, end use and a target market.

Primary colours have a full saturation or brightness and can be mixed to produce the widest number of colours. The primary colours are red, yellow and blue on the colour wheel, also referred to as RYB in the subtractive colour model. Their application in fashion terms is often as a highlight colour or accent colour; they offer vibrancy over any subtle qualities. They might also be used for active sportswear or for colour blocking, which is the juxtaposition of dominant, solid colours to create a striking graphic effect.

When two primary colours are mixed together they create secondary colours. This principle applies to both additive and subtractive colour mixing. Another six tertiary colours can be created by mixing primary and secondary colours with additional permutations thereafter.

Achromatic colours are those without hues: pure black, pure white and all shades of pure grey colour in between. In fashion design terms, achromatic colours play an important role and can be used on their own, in combination with each other or with chromatic colours. Of course, black and white are also complementary colours and are frequently used to offset each other in fashion design.

01 __ COLOUR ILLUSTRATION
Working with colour requires a sensitivity and understanding of how to create an appropriate mix and balance of colours across a collection or range.
Credit: Emma Brown

01

3.0 COLOUR AND FABRICS

Colour palettes

WORKING WITH COLOUR

Fashion designers are known for their seasonal colour palettes. This makes commercial sense as well as providing clarity and direction to a range or collection. Colour is often the first thing that you notice about a garment or design so its importance cannot be overstated. As we have seen, there are some scientific explanations for why certain colours work together in combination, such as complementary or analogous colours. These principles can be taught and will certainly enhance a fashion designer's understanding of how to put together colour palettes, either digitally or when selecting directly from the fabric or a colour swatch.

Working with colour in the context of fashion design is an intuitive experience, particularly when applying a particular colour to an individual garment. Consider, for example, how the same design might appear if it was presented in scarlet red and also in a cool grey. While the line, proportion and detail of both garments would be exactly the same, each might evoke a different response from a buyer or customer. In this way, we begin to understand that although colour can be constructed according to a set of rules, it remains an unpredictable and emotive element of fashion design. It is worth adding that there is no such thing as a bad colour; rather, it is the misuse of colour that can lead to design deficiencies.

While some fashion designers are associated with their bold use of colour (for example, Manish Arora), others choose to work with analogous or achromatic colours, such as black, white and grey (for example, Ann Demeulemeester). Either way, contemporary fashion designers will give careful consideration to the formulation of a colour palette in relation to target market, season and their signature style.

01—02 __ COLOUR CONCEPT BOARDS
Preparing and creating colour boards is a fundamental process for fashion designers to consider when preparing a collection. Colour can set the mood or tone for a collection with colour inspiration coming from any number of primary or secondary sources.
Credit: Mayya Cherepova

01

02

3.0 COLOUR AND FABRICS

SEASONAL PALETTES

In fashion design, colours are usually considered according to the seasons. This makes commercial sense but also in the context of applying colour to fabrics across a range of textures and weights where the absorption or reflection of light will ultimately affect the final quality of the colour. When considered across a collection of outfits, the trueness of the colour becomes very important. Any inconsistencies may appear as faults. Most fashion designers will select their colour palettes either from an open range offered by a textile mill at a fabric fair, such as Première Vision, or by developing lab-dips directly with textile mills.

Developing a seasonal colour palette takes time and is a rigorous process. The number of colours will vary but can be as little as three or four up to ten or more colours. Although multiple colours may be applied to a single garment through stripes or prints, the colour palette should be developed to work across the whole collection so that it offers multiple options to a customer. In this way the collection will not only be visually linked or coordinated but will also provide an opportunity to maximize sales.

Today, many fashion designers work with mills to develop colour palettes that are intensively researched in conjunction with international colour management and matching systems including Pantone and SCOTDIC. These systems span a variety of commercial industries, including fashion, interiors, plastics, architecture, paints and digital colours. They have enabled the use of colour palettes across different industries, which in turn has led to a more global outlook on colour that supports international colour forecasting organizations and industries.

01

COLOUR FORECASTING

Colour forecasting has become an established part of the fashion industry and the wider creative industries. It offers a logical approach to anticipating the seasonality of the fashion industry in response to a variety of external factors, including cultural and artistic movements, climate, politics, religion and technology.

Colour forecasting is not a dictate but rather a predictive indicator. The process involves detailed industry analysis and fashion trend spotting to reflect broad cultural influences and sector trends. Colour forecasts offer inspiration to fashion and textile professionals. Many textile companies employ colourists and range coordinators to manage colours across textile collections in conjunction with fashion designers.

A number of countries have established their own colour associations to aid the development of colour directions for domestic and export markets. These include the Color Association and Color Marketing Group in the US and the Society of Dyers & Colourists and British Textile Colour Group in the UK.

Textile and fabric trade shows including Première Vision in Paris, TexPrint and Pitti Immagine Filati in Italy are important industry platforms. They present colour forecasts to industry professionals who attend the biannual shows to meet with suppliers and confirm seasonal colour directions for their labels.

Additional trend and fashion lifestyle forecasting services, including Li Edelkoort, Trend Union, Peclers, Trendstop.com, The Donegar Group, Promostyl and others, offer global fashion reporting services that include colour analysis and fabric directions. These specialist industry services provide valuable insights, ideas and international viewpoints that augment the work of in-house design studios.

01 — COLOUR SIGNATURES
Working with print is a matter of choice for most fashion designers. For some, it can become a passion or even their signature style. London-based designer Mary Katrantzou presents a very personal view of print and was inspired by objects of desire including Fabergé eggs, Meissen porcelain and cloisonné enamel for her AW11 collection.
Credit: Catwalking

02 — FABRIC FAIRS
Fabric fairs such as Première Vision, and Heimtextil bring together fashion designers and buyers from all over the world to view new fabric collections and confirm trend directions.
Credit: Messe Frankfurt Exhibition GmbH/Pietro Sutera

02

Fibres

NATURAL FIBRES

Fibre is the basic structural element of a textile. It may be defined as any substance with a high length-to-width ratio that can be spun into a yarn or made into a fabric by bonding or interlacing in a variety of methods, including weaving, knitting, felting, twisting or braiding. Flax is considered to be one of the oldest fibres and has been used in the production of textiles since ancient times.

The classification of fibres is linked to type, length and size. Type refers to origin, such as whether a fibre is natural or man-made. Length refers to the dimensions of the fibre, of which there are three main classifications: short staple, long staple and continuous filament. Size refers to whether the fibre is ultra-fine, fine, regular or coarse.

Natural fibres make up a large group of textiles. This group includes any fibre that might be obtained from an animal, vegetable or mineral source that is capable of being converted into yarn.

Vegetable fibres may be derived from the trunk of a plant such as hemp palm; fruit and nut shells such as coconut; bast fibres, which have been removed from the stem of a plant such as linen, flax or jute; and fibres that are produced from the seed of a plant, such as cotton. Cotton and linen are the most important fibres used in fashion fabrics.

Cotton is a soft fibre that grows in the seed pod of the cotton plant. It is stronger when wet than dry, shrinks but is soft and strong, making it highly suitable for clothing. It absorbs moisture easily and takes dyes well.

Animal fibres consist largely of proteins and include hair, fur, wool and feathers. They can be further classified as staple fibres or filament fibres. Animal staple fibres include sheep's wool and speciality hair fibres such as alpaca or mohair.

The most common natural filament fibre is silk, which is obtained from the cocoon of the silkworm larva; it may be domestically cultivated, such as mulberry silk, or it may be wild. Silk is the longest and thinnest natural filament fibre. It is smooth, relatively soft and lustrous and also very strong. It is absorbent and accepts dyes readily.

Wool is derived from the fur of animals, principally sheep, of which there are many breeds. Each breed produces distinctive wools. Sheep's wool is one of the most important fibres used in textiles: it is easy to spin and when woven into fabric offers warmth and retains its shape. Wool also exhibits felting properties but absorbs dirt easily so should be kept clean. In addition to clothing some wools are used for carpets, felts, insulation and upholstery.

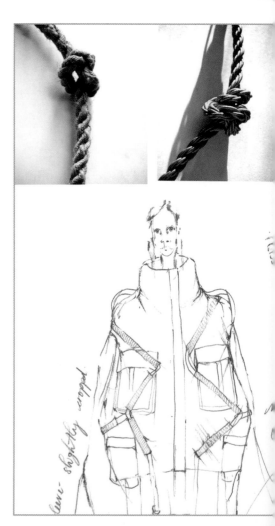

01—02 _ FABRIC RESEARCH
Colour and fabric development boards.
Credit: Lauren Sanins

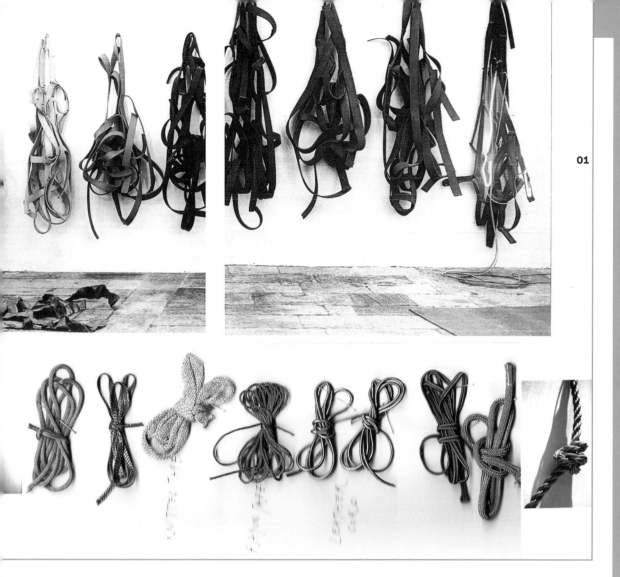

01

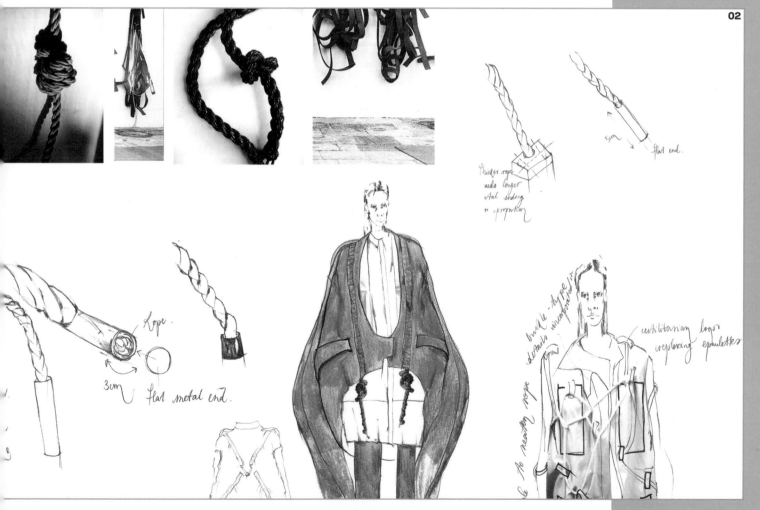

02

MANUFACTURED FIBRES

Manufactured fibres include two sub-classifications: cellulosic fibres and synthetic fibres. Cellulose is one of many polymers found in nature and it is used to produce rayon, acetate and triacetate.

Rayon was the first man-made fibre and is sometimes referred to as artificial silk. There are two principal varieties of rayon: viscose and cupra ammonium rayon or cupro. When woven into fabrics they have good draping properties, but are not suitable for pleating.

Acetate has a soft, lustrous appearance with draping properties and is resistant to wrinkles. It is also shrink resistant but it is a weak fibre so is often mixed with other fibres or used for linings. Special dyes have been developed for acetate as it does not respond to dyes used for cotton and rayon.

Synthetic fibres developed during the twentieth century have become an established part of textiles that are used in fashion. This classification includes many polymers that are used as fibres but most notably polyester and polyamide, also known as nylon and acrylic. Synthetic fibres offer an extended range of properties that make them suitable for use in sportswear clothing or for blending with natural fibres to enhance textile performance or durability. Synthetic fibres are typically smooth, hard-wearing and do not shrink.

FABRIC GUIDE BY FIBRE

Cotton	Wool	Silk	Man-made
Aertex	Alpaca	Barathea	Brocade
Brocade	Anglaise	Brocade	Chenille
Broderie	Angora	Chenille	Chiffon
Calico	Broadcloth	Chiffon	Cloqué
Candlewick	Brocade	Cloqué	Crêpe de Chine
Canvas	Camel hair	Crêpe de Chine	Crepon
Chenille	Casha	Crepon	Georgette
Chino	Challis	Dupion	Gold lamé
Chintz	Chenille	Faconne	Jersey
Cloqué	Cloqué	Faille	Ottoman
Corduroy	Doeskin	Georgette	Taffeta
Damask	Felt	Gold tissue	
Denim	Flannel	Jersey	
Gingham	Gaberdine	Marocain	
Jersey	Harris	Matelasse	
Lace	Herringbone	Moiré	
Lawn	Jersey	Organza	
Madras	Mohair	Ottoman	
Muslin	Moufflon	Petersham	
Net	Ottoman	Romain	
Organdie	Ratine	Surah	
Ottoman	Serge	Taffeta	
Percale	Sharkskin	Tulle	
Piqué	Velour		
Poplin	Venetian		
Sea island	Vicuna		
Seersucker	Worsted		
Terry towelling			
Velvet			

INNOVATIVE FIBRES

Rubber is a natural elastomer that has inspired the development of synthetic elastomeric fibres and brand names such as Lycra, Spandex and neoprene. These synthetic elastomeric fibres have transformed active sportswear and swimwear, combining comfort with high-performance attributes such as stretch and recovery. They are hugely significant in the evolution of fashion and ongoing developments in textile technology.

Some of the most inspiring developments in recent years include technological innovations such as Fabrican and LED fibres. Fabrican is a patented technology developed by Dr Manel Torres, a Royal College of Art fashion design graduate in collaboration with Imperial College London. Fabrican was marketed as the world's first spray-on fabric. London-based company CuteCircuit designs wearable technology, including garments with sensors, such as its award-winning Hug shirt, and LED lights woven into fibres to produce colour optical effects.

01

02

01 — GALAXY DRESS
The Galaxy Dress, created by London-based fashion company CuteCircuit, is the world's largest wearable LED display.
Credit: JB Spector, Museum of Science and Industry

02 — IRIS VAN HERPEN SS12
Designer Iris van Herpen uses unconventional materials such as metal and silk blends, burnt woven metals and shiny hair threads in her collections.
Credit: Lisa Galesloot

Fashion fabrics

WEAVE

Fabrics are made by spinning fibres into yarns that are woven, knitted or joined together into a pliable form. Some textiles are suitable for fashion design while others are manufactured for use as interior furnishings, carpets or industry. Understanding how to identify and select fashion fabrics is an essential part of being a fashion designer.

Understanding the characteristics of working with the grain is important in evaluating how to cut and drape the fabric. The 45° angle between the two grain-lines is known as the true bias of the fabric. Bias cutting and draping offers additional attributes that can be used to great effect.

Most fashion fabrics are either woven or knitted. Woven fabrics are produced on looms through a sequential process of interlacing or weaving two yarns together. Yarns that are set on the loom to run lengthwise down the length of the fabric are called warp yarns. The yarns that cross or fill the warps are called weft yarns or filling yarns and are set in place by a shuttle. As the shuttle passes back and forth it produces a finished edge called a selvedge. The finished lengthwise edge of the selvedge prevents the fabric from unravelling. The direction of the yarns in the fabric is known as the grain. The lengthwise grain follows the warp yarn while the crosswise grain follows the weft.

PLAIN WEAVE

A plain weave follows a simple interlacing system where the weft yarns interweave alternately under and over each warp yarn. From this basic configuration it is possible to produce a wide variety of fabrics with different textures, colours and settings. Variations of the plain weave include the rib weave, which produces a pronounced horizontal line across the fabric; cord weave, which produces a vertical line; and the hopsack weave, in which two filling yarns cross over and under pairs of warp yarns for a looser weave.

SATIN WEAVE

A satin weave produces a smooth fabric with a warp face. This is because each warp crosses over four or more filling yarns before passing under the fifth. Satin weave fabrics fray quite easily and have a defined right and wrong side. The right side is usually lustrous while the wrong side looks slightly coarse in comparison.

TWILL WEAVE

A twill weave fabric is characterized by a pronounced diagonal weave. The diagonal lines usually run down from right to left, although the reverse is called a left-hand twill. The angle of the diagonals can vary according to how many warp yarns float over wefts, while their prominence will be determined by the choice of yarn. Twill fabrics are hard-wearing but readily fray.

01 — NATURAL FIBRES
Natural fibres make up a large group of textiles that are obtained from an animal, vegetable or mineral source, spun into yarn and then made into fabric.
Credit: Messe Frankfurt Exhibition GmbH

01

KNIT

Where woven fabrics are constructed by interlacing at least two yarns, knitting is a process of converting yarn into fabric through a series of loops. Knitted fabric is made from either one continuous yarn or from a number of continuous yarns. Knitted fabrics can be constructed by hand or with a knitting machine. There are two main methods of knitting: weft knitting and warp knitting.

WEFT

Weft-knitted fabrics are made on knitting machines in which the yarn forms horizontal rows of loops across the fabric. They can be made either as flat or circular knits. Jersey fabrics are constructed using weft knitting and are available as single or double jersey knits. While jersey may sometimes offer the appearance of a soft woven fabric, it should be handled and sewn as a knitted fabric.

WARP

Warp-knitted fabrics are also made from interlocking loops. The knitting machine has a row of needles in the form of warp yarns, at least one warp yarn per needle. Each needle produces a chain of loops for each yarn in a warp direction, which is lengthwise along the fabric, but also loops through the stitch on each side. Warp knits do not ladder when cut and are generally firmer to sew with a limited amount of extensibility when compared to a weft knit.

ALTERNATIVE PROCESSES

Additional processes and techniques include quilting, where a layer of padding is inserted between two layers of fabric to create insulation. Quilted fabrics are usually finished with a decorative machine stitch. Bonding is another process that permanently laminates together two layers of fabric. The process is usually applied to performance fabrics where special features are required. Felt is an example of a non-woven fabric that might be used in fashion, which is constructed by matting, condensing and pressing fibres together. Felt does not have a grain or bias but can be shaped and stitched.

LACE

Additional methods of creating fabrics are largely based on a specific technique, technology or tradition. Laces and nets are examples of fabrics that are constructed by twisting, crossing or looping yarns into specific designs. Their open appearance makes them very distinctive. Lace was originally made by hand through a process of braiding and twisting lengths of threads around bobbins, known as bobbin lace, or by using a needle and thread to create a design known as needlelace. Most lace is now manufactured by machine, although its appearance remains distinctive and ornate.

FINISH

The handle of the fabric is determined by a combination of factors that include the texture of the yarn, the construction of the fabric and, importantly, the finish. Most fashion fabrics will be subjected to some form of finishing through their cycle of production. This could include chemical finishes to reduce shrinkage or to enhance softness, or water-repellent finishes such as silicone or wax. Mechanical finishing is sometimes applied to fabrics to stabilize them or alter the surface of the fabric through napping or brushing to raise the surface texture. Additional finishes might include anti-pilling, antimicrobial and anti-static or permanent press finishes. All finishes serve a specific purpose and can change the appearance and behaviour of a fabric, which should always be considered when selecting a fabric for a design.

In addition to functional finishes, many fashion fabrics are also the result of the aesthetic processes of dyeing and printing. Colour can be introduced at various stages in the production of a fabric. This might include dyeing the fibre, the yarn or the fabric (known as piece dyeing) or the final garment (known as garment or product dyeing).

Printing on fabric will significantly alter the visual appearance and character of a textile. Most fashion designers will select their print rather than produce them directly; however, it is useful to be able to distinguish between the variety of processes and printing techniques that exist today, which can broadly be divided between digital and non-digital prints. Working with prints and patterns can be an exhilarating experience for a fashion designer. For some designers the use of print or pattern can become a defining feature of their work.

01

**01 — FABRIC
SWATCHES**

Fashion designers will
usually collect fabric
swatches and begin
to arrange fabrics into
groups or themes.
This enables the
designer to compare
colours, textures and
weights of fabrics in
order to consider their
suitability and design
application.
*Credit: Messe
Frankfurt Exhibition
GmbH*

Designing for fabrics

FABRIC AWARENESS

The ability to design for a fabric is central to a fashion designer's work. It is important to develop an awareness and understanding for fabrics, which continues throughout a designer's career as technologies and finishes evolve. While many designers and fashion students will look for inspiration to start a collection, it is a knowledge and curiosity for fabrics, and what they can do when applied to the human form, that should inspire and motivate the practical work of a fashion designer.

The choice of fabric should be thoughtfully considered in relation to its end use. While it is understandable that many fashion students and designers set about trying to push boundaries and take risks, there is little point in trying to make a fabric perform against its inherent properties. In short, a fashion designer should always design with a fabric in mind.

The process of designing for fabrics begins with understanding how to identify and select a fabric. Fabric awareness is key to good design practice. Today, fashion designers are exposed to a huge variety of fabrics and finishes that should stimulate and enhance the creative process. Selecting the 'right' fabric should also be a tactile experience that engages the hand as well as the eye.

Most fashion designers and students will test their ideas in the studio through the production of a toile, also known as a muslin. These preliminary prototype forms should be made from a fabric that will be similar in weight, handle and construction to the intended final sample. If you intend to use a jersey fabric, for example, then your toile or muslin should also be in a jersey and not a woven calico.

Having already established the importance of testing your ideas and understanding the properties and characteristics of different fabrics, the process of selecting fabrics for sampling can be undertaken with consideration of structure, texture, weight, width, colour, finish and price.

The structure of a fabric should be observed and analysed to establish whether it is woven, knitted or constructed in another way. For woven and jersey fabrics, it is important to examine their structure: this will give you an early indication of how the fabric is likely to sew, as well as establishing its likely draping or tailoring properties. Examine both sides of the fabric to establish the right and the wrong side. This can also be determined by examining the selvedge. Some fabrics that are finished on both sides are classified as 'double-face' while most have a contrasting reverse side.

Recognizing and evaluating the texture of a fabric is a tactile process that begins with handling the fabric. You should feel the fabric to determine whether it is one that you would like to add to a collection or combine with other fabrics. The process of handling a fabric allows you to establish if the fabric has a distinctive handle such as a nap or a pile, in which case it will have to be cut as a one-way fabric. Some fabrics have distinctive weaves that appear like surface patterns or stripes. These will affect the way in which you can match it and cut out the fabric later.

WEIGHT

Establishing the weight of the fabric
is fundamental to the design process.
Although developing a knowledge of
fabric weights can help, the density of
the fabric will not always be revealed until
it is lifted up. You should therefore try to
lift up the approximate quantity of fabric
that you intend to use to see how heavy
or light it feels. This will also enable you
to test the fabric's draping or tailoring
properties before you commit to buying it.

FABRIC QUESTIONS

How does the fabric 'hand' or
handle?

What is the fabric suitable for?

Is the fabric made from natural
fibres, man-made fibres or a
combination of both? Remember
that the fibre composition will be an
important guide to how the fabric
will perform.

How does the fabric drape?

How is the fabric likely to sew?

Will the fabric shrink, fray or
stretch?

Is the fabric finished to a
performance specification? If so,
what will this mean when sewing it
later? Some chemical finishes may
enhance the performance of the
fabric but may require extra sewing
and handling skills.

Should the fabric be washed or
dry-cleaned? This is also important
in evaluating the choice.

FABRIC WEIGHTS REFERENCE TABLE

OUNCES PER RUNNING YARD	GRAMS PER RUNNING METRE	GRAMS PER SQUARE METRE
6-7oz	185-220g	120-140g
7-8oz	220-250g	140-160g
8-9oz	250-280g	160-180g
9-10oz	280-310g	180-200g
10-11oz	310-340g	200-220g
11-12oz	340-370g	220-240g
12-13oz	370-400g	240-260g
13-14oz	400-435g	260-280g
14-15oz	435-465g	280-300g
15-16oz	465-495g	300-320g
16-17oz	495-525g	320-340g
17-18oz	525-560g	340-360g
18-19oz	560-590g	360-380g
19-20oz	590-620g	380-400g

WIDTH

Fabric widths can vary so it is important to check the width of the fabric before you buy it. This will directly affect how you can cut the fabric later. Long-fitting bias-cut designs, for example, usually require full width fabrics. Establishing the width should also be considered it relation to the price of the fabric. Narrow widths may appear less expensive until you realize how much meterage or yardage you need to buy. Fabric widths can vary from around 90cm for some shirtings, up to 150cm for most fashion fabrics. Linings are frequently available in narrow widths so always check the width before you buy any fabric.

01 — FIBRE DIAGRAM
Understanding fibre classifications will greatly assist fashion designers in making informed choices when sourcing and selecting fabrics. It will also indicate a fabric's likely properties and dyeing capabilities.

> Man needs colour to live; it's just as necessary an element as fire and water.

FERNAND LÉGER

01

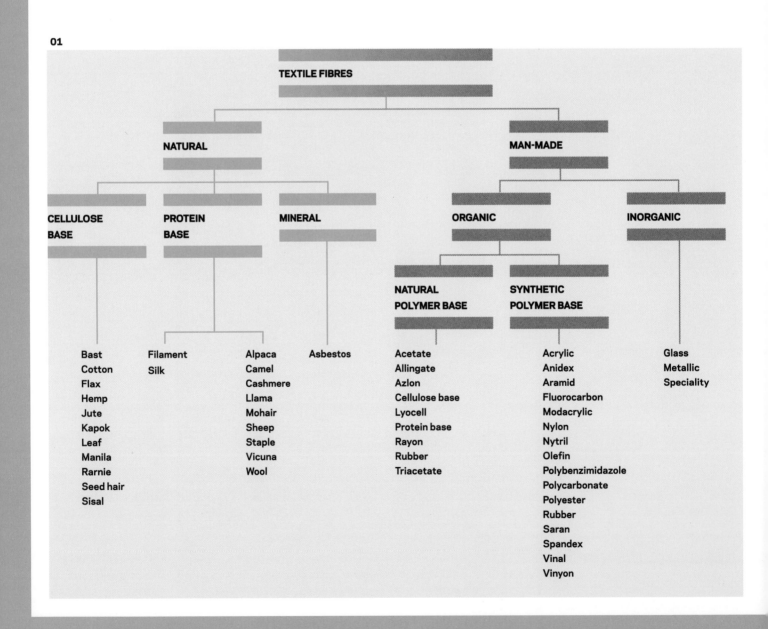

TEXTILE FIBRES

NATURAL

MAN-MADE

CELLULOSE BASE

PROTEIN BASE

MINERAL

ORGANIC

INORGANIC

NATURAL POLYMER BASE

SYNTHETIC POLYMER BASE

Bast	Filament	Alpaca	Asbestos	Acetate	Acrylic	Glass
Cotton	Silk	Camel		Allingate	Anidex	Metallic
Flax		Cashmere		Azlon	Aramid	Speciality
Hemp		Llama		Cellulose base	Fluorocarbon	
Jute		Mohair		Lyocell	Modacrylic	
Kapok		Sheep		Protein base	Nylon	
Leaf		Staple		Rayon	Nytril	
Manila		Vicuna		Rubber	Olefin	
Rarnie		Wool		Triacetate	Polybenzimidazole	
Seed hair					Polycarbonate	
Sisal					Polyester	
					Rubber	
					Saran	
					Spandex	
					Vinal	
					Vinyon	

COLOUR

Colour is one of the most emotive elements in design, so it is important when choosing fabrics to establish colour trueness. Fabrics should always be viewed and compared in good natural light or using a controlled light box viewer. In as much as you would expect to find variations of pigment colours, not all blacks or whites are the same either. Selecting the desired colour for a design is a combination of personal choice, market requirements and the designer's colour palette. Colour has an immediate impact in any collection, so whether you are working from a colour card, working with a mill to create lab dips or buying your fabric directly from a retailer, it should be given critical attention as it will ultimately communicate your design.

02 __ FABRIC FAIRS
Specialist fabric and yarn trade fairs offer fashion designers the chance to review and discuss colours and prints with suppliers and manufacturers. These trade shows are important seasonal fixtures in the fashion calendar.
Credit: Messe Frankfurt Exhibition GmbH/Pietro Sutera

02

FINISH

PRICE

As discussed earlier, fabric finishes can vary enormously and include a variety of chemical and mechanical finishes. These may include brushed finishes and aesthetic finishes, such as printing, flocking, foiling and pleating. Each finish will have its own distinct attributes and characteristics. In turn, these will directly affect the handling properties and suitability of the fabric for its intended design use. It is also important to establish what the care or special sewing requirements might be as well as testing the fabric through a sample unit or design studio to be assured that it works in the way that is intended.

The price of a fabric should be understood in relation to a number of commercial factors. This includes whether the fabric is being purchased at cost, wholesale or retail price. Additional taxes and shipping costs may also apply. Most commercial designers will be guided by the costing and pricing structure within their business or organization. In reality, even if a fabric has been chosen and sampled by a designer it may not always be possible to offer it within a collection if it proves to be too expensive when priced up through a factory unit. Fashion students are advised to compare the prices of comparable qualities by visiting retail competitors or direct wholesalers. The quality of fabrics should be consistent within a collection and, while there will be price variations, they must ultimately be considered in relation to the cost of each garment to produce a fully costed collection.

Start collecting fabric swatches throughout your studies and build up a reference source from which you can make informed decisions to support your fabric awareness and design development. It is worth remembering that all fashion designs are expressed and presented through the designer's choice of fabrics.

01

3.0 COLOUR AND FABRICS

01 — SWATCHES
It is useful to collect fabric swatches to gain an understanding of the variety of fashion fabrics available. Maintaining a fabric swatch book will assist in identifying and preparing collections.
Credit: Remi

Q&A
Lauretta Roberts

Name

Lauretta Roberts

Occupation

Creative director at WGSN Boutique

Website

www.wgsn.com

Biography

Lauretta Roberts is creative director of WGSN Boutique, the arm of global fashion trend forecaster WGSN that is dedicated to independent retail. She is also director of the WGSN Global Fashion Awards, which take place in New York in the autumn – she launched this initiative for WGSN in 2010.

Prior to joining WGSN, Lauretta was at its sister business *Drapers*, the UK's fashion industry title, of which she is still editor. A digital advocate, Lauretta launched Drapers' first content website and added to its portfolio of live events with the Drapers' Etail Awards.

Can you tell us about WGSN Boutique and what it does?

WGSN Boutique is just a part of WGSN, which is the world's leading fashion trend forecaster. The Boutique trends are specific to independent retailers but our main business for WGSN is global brands and retailers – we have about 38,000 users in 57 countries.

How do you prepare your trend guides?

We have a number of different types. Each season, about two years ahead, we prepare our three macro trends, which set the scene for the season. These are based on evidence collated by our global team of experts who meet in London to call and shape the trends.

They start out being about direction, colour and mood but become more tangible collections as we draw closer to the season.

We also do trend reports based on street fashion, in-store product, catwalks, trade shows and cultural movements in, say, film, art and celebrity.

Why do trends matter in the fashion industry?

They keep it moving and they keep us in jobs! You have to give people new reasons to buy new clothes. Sometimes those are dramatic reasons; sometimes they are subtle.

But fashion trends don't exist in isolation; they're at the centre of broader cultural movements and reflect the changes to the way we live. Fashion has to change to remain relevant.

Should fashion designers set the trends or follow them?

It depends on your job; if you're a designer at a high-street retailer, then your job is very much following trends, but you need to know which ones to back, in which way and at what time, depending on your customer. And that's a very creative job, which requires great judgement.

At the other end of the scale, there are designers you look to for redefinition of fashion or new ideas and touches; Miuccia Prada is one of those, she's always ahead of the curve. But younger designers too, like Erdem, have been very influential recently.

How is technology affecting the way in which trends are identified and communicated to clients?

It's made the world so much faster and so much smaller. The consumer has access to trends at the same time as the industry – sometimes they're on it before – and that places pressure on the industry to deliver the right product faster. It makes researching trends easier, but although we're an online business, our people are still very much out there on the ground and I don't think you can replace that.

What do you love most about your job?

A hard question. I love the Global Fashion Awards the most, but I also love looking at what the team here wear every day. If I'm not sure of a trend I look around me, and if they're not wearing it then it makes me think twice.

01

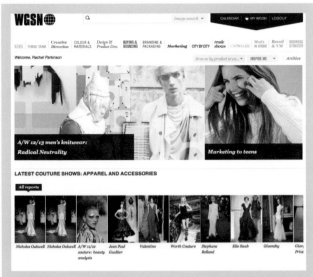

01 — WGSN
As the fashion industry becomes increasingly exposed to the gaze and scrutiny of savvy consumers and industry professionals, the need to understand and distinguish between a fad or a trend has become more important than ever.
Credit: WGSN

01

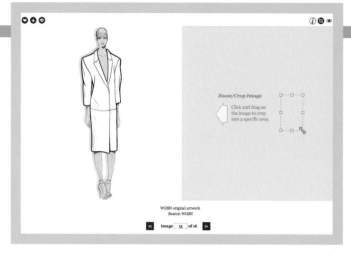

WGSN original artwork
Source: WGSN

image 13 of 16

The Y gilet

Y_gilet.eps

- Dramatic top-heavy gilet with a primordial feel. The curving shoulderline forms wide, grown-on sleeves, while the body tapers towards the hem and is belted low on the hips

S/S 13 MACRO TRENDS

By WGSN Creative team, 11 July 2011

Index   WonderLab   The Story of Now   Idiomatic

Spring/summer 2013 Macro Trends

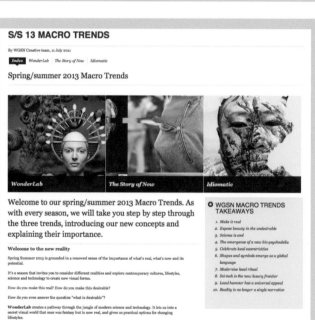

Welcome to our spring/summer 2013 Macro Trends. As with every season, we will take you step by step through the three trends, introducing our new concepts and explaining their importance.

Welcome to the new reality

Spring Summer 2013 is grounded in a renewed sense of the importance of what's real, what's now and its potential.

It's a season that invites you to consider different realities and explore contemporary cultures, lifestyles, science and technology to create new visual forms.

How do you make this real? How do you make this desirable?

How do you even answer the question "what is desirable"?

WonderLab creates a pathway through the jungle of modern science and technology. It lets us into a secret visual world that once was fantasy but is now real, and gives us practical options for changing lifestyles.

WGSN MACRO TRENDS TAKEAWAYS

1. Make it real
2. Expose beauty in the undesirable
3. Science is cool
4. The emergence of a new bio-psychedelia
5. Celebrate local eccentricities
6. Shapes and symbols emerge as a global language
7. Modernise local ritual
8. Sci-tech is the new luxury frontier
9. Local humour has a universal appeal
10. Reality is no longer a single narrative

WGSN store shot, Harar, Ethiopia

Missoni spring/summer 2011

WGSN street shot, St-Tropez
Source: WGSN

image 5 of 70

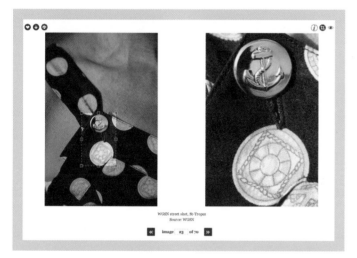

WGSN street shot, St-Tropez
Source: WGSN

image 23 of 70

WGSN street shot, St-Tropez
Source: WGSN

image 25 of 70

01 — WGSN

WGSN has established itself as a major online resource to businesses, designers and fashion students. Its range of subscription services provide creative intelligence and ideas to assist style-related businesses, as well as analysing macro trends and covering all the major fashion week events with city-by-city analysis and streetstyle reports.
Credit: WGSN

Max Aria pre-summer 2012   WGSN original artwork   Source: As seen at www.patternity.com

Discussion questions
Activities
Further reading

DISCUSSION QUESTIONS

ACTIVITIES

DISCUSSION QUESTIONS

1 Identify and select colour images from fashion collections. Evaluate and discuss their colour palettes with consideration to the identified fabrics.

2 Discuss how fabrics contribute to contemporary fashion design, with reference to established practices and new technologies.

3 Collect a variety of fabrics. Identify their structure and fibre compositions and discuss their potential design applications.

ACTIVITIES

1 Select an artwork that inspires you and create a seasonal colour palette using a recognized colour matching system. Present it with consideration for seasonal and market requirements.

2 Identify a fashion label or brand and analyse its seasonal fabric selection. Create a fabric storyboard for your chosen label and link this to a theme and colour palette as the basis for a limited-edition capsule collection.

3 Collect a variety of fashion fabric swatches. Analyse each fabric's handling properties and fibre composition. Produce a series of sketches for your fabrics to demonstrate your understanding of each fabric's potential use.

FURTHER READING

The empires of the future are the empires of the mind. **WINSTON CHURCHILL**

Baugh, G
The Fashion Designer's Textile Directory: The Creative Use of Fabrics in Design
Thames & Hudson, 2011

Braddock Clarke, S & O'Mahony, M
Techno Textiles 2: Revolutionary Fabrics for Fashion and Design: Bk2
Thames & Hudson, 2007

Colchester, C
Textiles Today: A Global Survey of Trends and Traditions
Thames & Hudson, 2009

Cole, D
Textiles Now
Laurence King, 2008

Collier, B; Bide, M & Tortora, T
Understanding Textiles
Pearson Education (7th ed), 2008

Holtzsche, L
Understanding Color: an Introduction for Designers
John Wiley & Sons (4th ed), 2011

Quinn, B
Textile Futures: Fashion, Design and Technology
Berg, 2010

Tortora, P & Merkel. R
Fairchild's Dictionary of Textiles
Fairchild Books, 1996

Wilson, J
Classic and Modern Fabrics: The Complete Illustrated Sourcebook
Thames & Hudson, 2010

Wolff, C
The Art of Manipulating Fabric
Krause Publications (2nd ed), 1996

The Color Association
www.colorassociation.com

Color Marketing Group
www.colormarketing.org

The Doneger Group
www.donegar.com

Pantone Inc
www.pantone.com

Peclers Paris
www.peclersparis.com

Pitti Immagine Filati
www.pittimmagine.com

Première Vision
www.premierevision.com

Promostyl
www.promostyl.com

SCOTDIC – the World Textile Color System
www.scotdic.com

Society of Dyers and Colourists
www.sdc.org.uk

Texprint
www.texprint.org.uk

The Textile Institute
www.texi.org

Trendstop
www.trendstop.com

Tissu Premier
www.tissu-premier.com

4.0 CONCEPT TO PROTOTYPE

OBJECTIVES

To become familiar with the layout and main equipment used in a fashion design sample studio

To understand the main principles of flat pattern making and draping

To understand the function and purpose of creating a toile/muslin

To consider the roles of fit and sizing in fashion design

To identify popular sewing techniques and practices used in fashion design

To appreciate the context of a prototype sample in fashion design

01 — TOILE
A toile/muslin usually represents the first expression of a designer's concept as a physical prototype. Most toiles are made from undyed calico fabric to enable the designer to review and evaluate the three-dimensional form prior to cutting into the final fabric or adding colour and trimmings.
Credit: Laura Helen Searle

01

The fashion studio

The fashion studio is a dedicated working environment in which the fashion designer tests and explores ideas. The basic function of a design studio or sample room is to enable the designer to produce a prototype or final sample. It will usually include most of the following resources:

A variety of **industrial sewing machines** capable of sewing woven and knitted fabrics. Stitch varieties might include a chain stitch, lock stitch, multi-thread chain stitch, over-edge stitch (also called an overlock stitch), covering stitch and a safety stitch.

Domestic sewing machines are sometimes used, with capabilities that include a zigzag stitch or an adjustable domestic buttonhole stitch.

A **fusing press** for bonded interfacings, with a safety cut-off switch.

Adequate **steam presses** and **steam irons** with safe access to a water supply. Some steam presses have vacuum capabilities to hold garments in place as they are being pressed.

A variety of **dress stands**, also referred to as dress forms or 'dummies'. These are produced by specialist companies such as Kennett & Lindsell and Stockman who supply the fashion industry with either standardized or custom-made stands. Dress stands are designed to replicate the human form to a required size. They are available for menswear, womenswear and childrenswear as either torso forms, skirt or trouser forms or as fully bifurcated forms with torso and legs. Some dress stands have collapsible shoulders while others can have an arm attachment for modelling sleeves.

An appropriate allocation of **cutting tables** for the size of the studio. These will be used for producing flat patterns or for laying out and cutting fabric.

Garment rails for holding samples. These should be on casters for easy mobility.

Supply of **pattern paper** or card stock for producing sample patterns.

Metric rulers for measuring. These are usually made of aluminium and need to be durable and accurate.

Fixing weights for laying on to patterns to hold them in place.

A **mirror** in the studio to view samples on a human figure.

Additional equipment should include a **flexible tape measure, pattern paper notchers, steel dressmaking pins, tailor's shears** for cutting fabric and **paper scissors** for cutting paper (these two should not be mixed up), **tailor's chalk, style tape, stitch ripper, needle point tracing wheel, hard pencils, eraser** and a personal **pattern master ruler, French curve ruler** or measuring Perspex set-square with 45° and 90° angles.

01 — EQUIPMENT
A Tape measure
B Cutting shears
C Steel pins
D Paper scissors
E Thread snips and lightweight scissors
F Transparent pattern drawing aid (pattern-master shown)
G Transparent set square
H Tracing wheel
I Metal metre rule
J Pattern notcher
K Masking tape
L Stitch unpicker
M Bobbin and bobbincase
N Tailor's chalk
O Pattern block (bodice block shown)
P Selection of sewing machine feet
Credit: Alison Wescott

02 — DESIGN STUDIO
The fashion design studio is typical of many college sample studios. It is equipped with industrial sewing machines positioned close to natural light as well as cutting tables and sample-size dress forms. Fashion design students share these common work spaces to produce toiles and first samples.

01

02

Sizing and measurements

Sizing and measurements are inextricably linked to a number of processes in fashion design. Taking a measurement is an important step in creating a prototype sample in the design studio; however, it should not to be confused with sizing, which has a broader role that includes pattern grading and classifying measurements for commercial manufacturing and retailing.

Attempts have been made to organize the sizing of clothes into nationally recognized values, such as the National Sizing Survey in the UK and the Department of Commerce in the USA. International variations remain, however. Europe, follows a metric system whereas the USA is imperial. These measurements form the basis of national standard sizing systems, which are subject to periodic sizing surveys. Size surveys have shown that the average male and female figure changes over time and that measurements based on the average woman during the 1950s no longer reflect the average size of a woman today. When age, ethnicity and lifestyle are factored in, it becomes increasingly evident that sizing schemes present national characteristics whilst simultaneously evolving over time.

In the UK, the National Sizing Survey utilized 3D whole body scanners to produce accurate sizing data. Using advanced technologies from Sizemic, a London-based fashion technology company, the survey involved taking 130 body measurements from 11,000 human subjects in standing and seated positions. The results identified significant body size variations from previous recorded data.

Sizing can also be associated with clothing sectors. Many casual clothing lines are sized up as small, medium and large; children's clothes are sized by age. Formal clothing, including business suits for men and women are sized by numeric ratios. In menswear it is common practice to offer additional fittings across the same size, such as short, regular and long. Bespoke or custom-made clothes, such as exclusive evening and bridalwear might be individually sized to a customer's specifications. In this way, we can also recognize that the sizing of clothes is further affected by the relationship between cut, fit and shape.

From a fashion design perspective, a jacket may be cut to have a loose fit or a slim fit, but both could carry the same size label. While attempting to offer perspectives on sizing, fashion designers and design students are likely to work on a dress stand in a chosen sample size. This is usually a size 10 or 12 in the UK and 8 or 10 in the US for women and a size 38 or 40 for menswear. Understanding how to take measurements is fundamental in the process of transferring an idea to a three-dimensional sample, either through a flat pattern or draping process.

Listed below are the main body measurements that are applied to womenswear:

- Bust size
- Waist size
- Hip size
- Nape of neck to waist or hip
- Waist to hip or knee
- Shoulder from the neck point
- Neck to wrist length
- Wrist
- Body rise for trousers (taken in the seated position)
- Front and back rise (for trousers/pants)
- Inside leg measurement

Most college design studios will have a set of dress stands and a corresponding set of pattern blocks, called slopers in the US, which correspond with the measurements of the dress stands. These ensure that the block will fit the stand and allow the designer to work more efficiently, without the need to make modifications to the block before using it to develop a first sample.

01

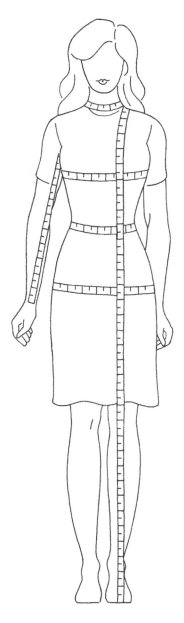
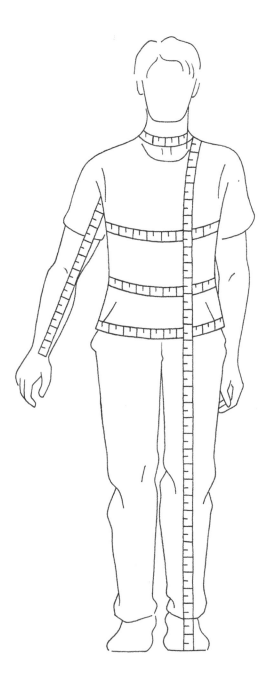

01 ＿ MEASURING

Taking measurements
is a fundamental
part of preparing flat
patterns and samples.
It is important to also
include ease and seam
allowances on most
sample patterns.
Credit: Penny Brown

Pattern making

SAMPLE PATTERN

BLOCKS

Pattern making broadly describes the process of creating and adapting shapes to translate a two-dimensional design into a three-dimensional form. The process requires a combination of technical skills and the ability to visualize three dimensions. The shaped pattern pieces are made into a prototype garment called a toile or muslin. Developing a flat pattern into a garment should always take account of height, width and girth.

For most fashion designers, pattern making simultaneously encompasses the technical process of cutting an accurate pattern and the creative interpretation of a design source such as a fashion sketch. In the fashion industry, pattern making also reflects costing and manufacturing requirements. The first pattern that is created in a sample room or design studio is called a sample pattern. This type of pattern might be drafted on paper or lightweight card but requires further 'engineering' in order to become a production pattern. Production patterns are fully styled patterns that are transferred on to firm card for manufacturing purposes. They need to be highly durable and suitable for grading up or down into the required number of sizes, known as a nest of grades. They also include all seam allowances, notches, grain-lines, size, style name or code and cutting instructions.

Fashion students will be more familiar with blocks or **slopers**. These patterns are generic rather that styled and do not include seam allowances. A fashion block is based on a standard measuring system and may be referred to simply as a bodice, skirt or trouser block. Bodice blocks may be altered according to fit characteristics such as bust darts. While they form the basis of a shape from which a styled design can be drafted and developed into a prototype sample, basic blocks need to be distinguished between those that apply to woven fabrics and others that have been developed for knitted or stretch fabrics, such as jersey, as they will have different tolerances.

Sloper
A sloper is the US term for a block, which is used as the basis for drafting a styled pattern.

01 — BLOCK
Flat patterns should accommodate circumferential breadth as well as height and width. Designers are therefore required to consider the back and side views of each design.

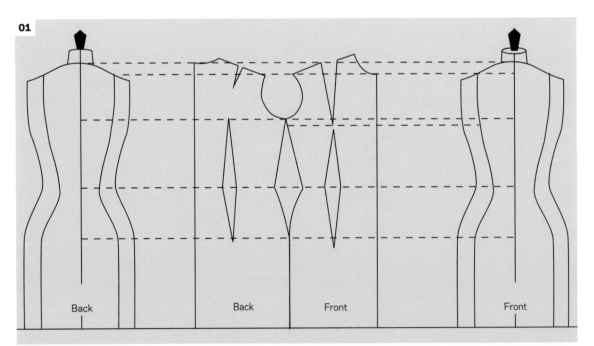

01

Back   Back   Front   Front

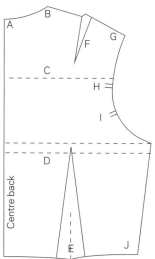

1/4 SCALE BODICE   **1/4 SCALE FRONT BODICE**

1/4 SCALE SLEEVE

A	Nape	1	Back pitch (sleeve)
B	Neck point	2	Shoulder point
C	Across back	3	Sewing notch
D	Bust line	4	Front pitch
E	Back waist dart	5	Bicep line
F	Shoulder dart	6	Sewing notch
G	Shoulder point	7	Back arm line
H	Back pitch	8	Centre line (sleeve)
I	Sewing notch	9	Forearm line
J	Waistline	10	Elbow line
K	Sewing notch	11	Underarm seam
L	Front pitch	12	Wrist line
M	Bust dart	13	Elbow dart
N	Bust point		
O	Front waist dart		
P	Neck gorge		

02 — STYLE LINES
Bust and waist darts can be closed into seam lines in a variety of different ways to become style lines, offering plenty of creative opportunities.

03 — DART MANIPULATION
Understanding the principle of dart suppression is an important stage in taking a pattern from a 2D drawing to a 3D prototype.

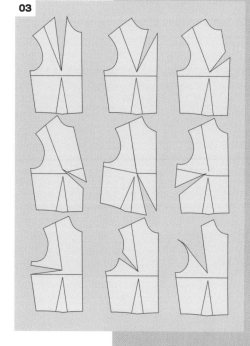

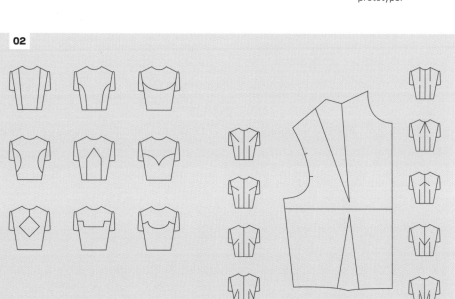

DRAFTING A PATTERN

A pattern is traced from the block to allow the designer to start applying design features such as seams, gathers or pleats. In the industry, the process of creating a first pattern is usually undertaken by a skilled pattern maker, but it still needs to be fully understood by the fashion designer. This process usually starts with the designer's sketch or working drawing. This should include a back view, with all style lines clearly indicated. The next stage is to select the appropriate block; working from the wrong block will only delay the process and may result in the wrong fit. Use a sharp pencil, such as a 2H, to prepare the pattern. Accuracy is very important as any deviations will result in a pattern that doesn't fit together. Using a set square or curve can be helpful, otherwise all lines should be carefully drawn by hand. Understanding dart manipulation and techniques of pivoting the block to move suppression is critical to producing many patterns that accentuate the form. Adding fullness can also be achieved through 'slash' and pattern spreading techniques.

All the pattern pieces are then traced off using a tracing wheel, and each piece should be clearly labelled and marked with grain-lines, notches and cutting instructions. Seam allowances need to be considered before cutting out the pieces. These may vary according to their required function.

SUMMARY PATTERN CUTTING NOTES FOR STUDENTS

Always use a sharp pencil, preferably 2H or similar. Softer pencils do not produce accurate lines

Always measure and draw all lines accurately, especially seam allowances

Use a pattern master or Perspex set-square with 45° and 90° angles, to make sure that right angles and bias lines are accurate

Create a pattern draft. You can refer to this for alterations later if necessary

Pattern pieces should fit together so always check them before cutting out

Your pattern should be appropriate to your intended fabric

Make sure openings and fastenings are marked on your patterns

Always choose the correct block for a design

Consult your own notes or reference books for more advanced cutting

Make a toile/muslin to evaluate the fit and style of your pattern

Mark any alterations on to your toile then transfer these to your pattern and adjust as necessary

Make sure that you produce clear working drawings before you start cutting a pattern

Include all relevant information on all your pattern pieces such as grain-lines, balance notches, size of pattern, pattern style and cutting instructions, such as seam allowances and the number of pieces to be cut or folded

Keep all patterns pieces together, including your draft for further reference

01

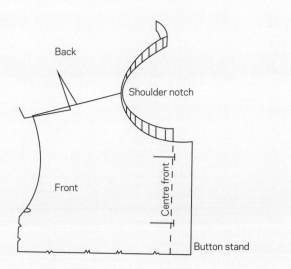

01—02 _ COLLAR STAND

Drafting a collar stand involves taking a series of neckline measurements, establishing the centre-front position of a garment and adding a button stand. Many collars are constructed as two pieces: the stand supports the collar and should be drafted to fit comfortably around the neck.

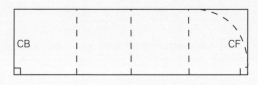

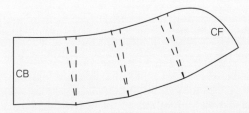

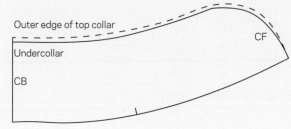

02

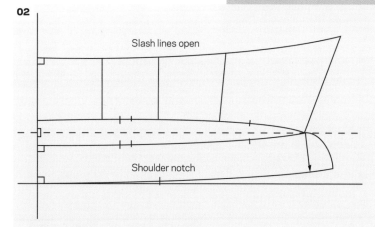

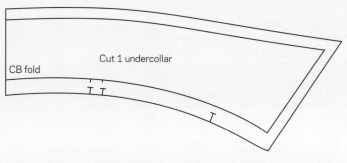

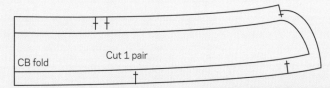

Draping

Draping offers an alternative method of creating a pattern by working directly on the stand with fabric. It offers immediate results but requires a level of dexterity and manipulative skills, which can be taught and developed with practice. For some designers this is a more intuitive process; one that can help to confirm the visualization process needed to realize a three-dimensional form.

Draping does not reflect usual methods of production in industry but does offer a designer the creative experience of exploring the relationship between shape and fit. It can be readily applied to a variety of woven and knitted fabrics and used to create fitted shapes as well as to drape fullness around the body. It is more usually applied to womenswear than to menswear; in particular, bias-cut styles, eveningwear, bridalwear and experimental shapes where immediate results can be obtained.

Before draping, it is important to select your dress stand carefully and make sure that it offers the correct shape and balance. The stand should be clearly marked with the bust, waist and hip positions. The draping process is informed by the choice of fabric and whether you intend to work with straight grain, a crosswise grain or bias, or the true 45° bias, which offers distinct draping qualities.

Before working directly on the stand the fabric should be carefully examined for any flaws. It should then be prepared for draping by marking on the centre-front grain-line and the bust line. Some fabrics will need to be pressed before they can be used to remove unnecessary creases or eliminate possible shrinkage. Make sure you are using good-quality pins and that you have a sharp pair of shears or dressmaking scissors.

When working directly on the stand it is crucial to understand balance. This refers to the hang of the draped material. Whether you are working with the straight grain or the bias, your design should be balanced without any unplanned dragging, twisting or pulling of the fabric. These signs will indicate an imbalance that should be addressed before continuing with the drape.

The alignment of the straight grain to the centre-front and the crosswise grain to the hem is sometimes referred to as the 'plumb theory' and is associated with dropping a plumb line to determine the vertical suspension of weight. Only when the stand is prepared and the fabric applied in alignment should the process of draping begin.

Most fashion design students will be introduced to draping through the basic bodice. This is the process of draping a fitted form using darts to create suppression around the bodice and understanding the relationship between the apex, that is the fullest part of the bust and the waist, shoulders and side seams, which should all be aligned in the finished toile/muslin. As the bodice is being draped all measuring points should be accurately recorded and marked, such as the neckline, armhole scye and length of each dart. Once completed the fabric is removed from the stand and laid flat so that all the markings can be transferred on to pattern paper using a tracing wheel. It is a skilled process that requires accuracy and patience, but it is a useful platform from which to develop further styles, either through additional draping or by using the draped pattern as the basis for a flat pattern draft.

01 — DRAPING
This 3D development board illustrates a series of draping processes. Draping is an alternative method for creating a pattern. Draping requires applied technical skills and accuracy, enabling the designer to experiment with shapes and evaluate proportions.
Credit: Laura Helen Searle

The convention is that you start from a flat fabric cut out on a surface, but that, to me, has nothing to do with the body. **KOJI TATSUNO**

01

3D Development... THREE

Tinker Tailor Soldier Spy
Laura Helen Searle
Final Collection 2011

Sewing

HAND SEWING

Sewing involves joining, assembling and stitching fabrics, as well as measuring, marking, cutting and pressing. Most fashion design students will be familiar with the term 'press as you go', which refers to pressing in conjunction with sewing.

Sewing is a skilled operation with established rules and practices. As with most skills, it can be improved with practice and requires close attention and accuracy. In the fashion industry, many designers and design studios employ sample machinists to make a complete sample from cut work. Cut work is a design that has been cut out in fabric from a pattern and includes a specification sheet or sketch from which the sample machinist can assemble the design. Fashion design students are usually expected to sew their own samples and will certainly learn from the experience. Most designers will not be required to commercially sew their own designs in industry, but they will need to oversee the process.

Hand sewing is a tactile process that covers **basting**, tacking, hemming and decorative stitch work, including embroidery. Working in good light is essential. The type of needle used will vary depending on the sewing operation and fabric. Sharps hand-sewing needles can be used for general-purpose sewing and are available in a range of sizes. Ball-points should be used for knitted fabrics. Leather and embroidery both require special needles.

Basting
Basting refers to a temporary stitch that is used to join or hold edges or garment pieces together. It is applied without tension and removed from a final sample or garment.

RUNNING STITCH

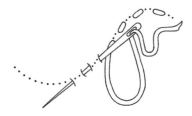

Running stitch is used for basting to hold two or more fabrics together. It is a good introductory stitch for beginners.

SLIP STITCH

MARKING TACKS

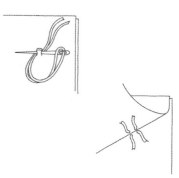

Slip stitch is an almost invisible stitch that is formed by slipping the fabric under a clean fold of fabric such as a hem or waistband.

Marking tacks are used to transfer sewing assembly details and matching points from a pattern on to the fabric.

BACKSTITCH

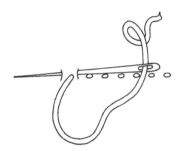

Backstitch is one of the strongest and most versatile stitches. It can be used to reinforce or repair a seam. It can look like a machine lock stitch.

PRICK STITCH

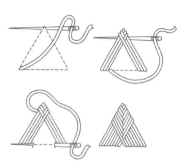

Prick stitch is a variation of the backstitch but is made without catching the underlayer of the fabric. It is used mainly as a decorative topstitching.

ARROWHEAD TACK

Arrowhead tack has a distinctive triangular appearance. It serves as a reinforcement stitch at strain points, such as the corner of a pocket or the end of an inverted pleat.

BLIND STITCH

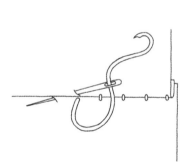

Blind stitch is worked inside, between the hem and the garment, so that it is not visible and the edge of the hem does not press into the garment.

FEATHER STITCH

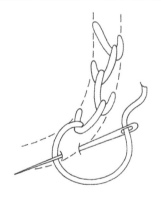

Feather stitch is a decorative stitch with a distinctive appearance where the stitches are taken on alternate sides of a given line.

BAR TACK

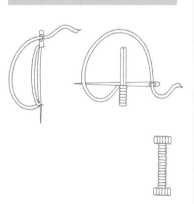

Bar tack is a straight reinforcement stitch that is used at points of strain. This might include the ends of a buttonhole or the corner of a pocket.

MACHINE SEWING

Machine sewing involves operating an industrial or domestic sewing machine. All sewing machines need to be top-threaded to a spool, which is threaded through tension discs and on to a needle, and bottom-threaded on to a bobbin, which fits inside a bobbin case. The settings between the upper and lower threads should be established at the correct tension so that the stitches are evenly balanced in response to the foot pedal and feed dog when the fabric passes under the presser foot. Both threads pass under the presser foot in readiness to start the sewing operation. It is useful to familiarize yourself with the component parts of a sewing machine, then stitch a series of parallel lines in order to acquire the necessary 'feel' and control of the machine. All sewing machines have their own feel but with practice they will respond to the operator.

It is important to use a suitable needle for the type of fabric. Knitted fabrics such as jersey should be sewn with a ball-point needle while woven fabrics may be sewn with a sharp-point needle or extra fine-point needle. Sewing leather requires a leather needle, which has a sharpened triangular point. Needle sizes vary, so always check before you start to sew your fabric. As a guide, the finer the yarn, the finer the needle. Stitch lengths should also be considered in relation to the weight, structure and texture of the fabric. Threads should also be selected with care. Spun polyester threads are the most versatile but check before you sew. Embroidery and topstitching require different threads. Sewing machines are fitted with a variety of sewing feet. These may need to be changed depending on the sewing operation but can include a zipper foot, buttonhole foot, felling foot, gather foot, Teflon foot for sewing leather, tailor tacking foot, embroidery foot and a straight stitch foot.

GENERAL INFORMATION

Test out a sample length of your chosen fabric before you sew it. This includes pressing the fabric to see how it reacts

Think about the type of seams you will need as part of your design. These will vary according to the method of manufacture, chosen fabric and the type of garment. All seams should be identified and considered at the design stage

Consider all edge finishes including hems. These will also vary according to the desired manufacture, fabric and garment design

Think about all facings and openings as part of your design. These should be sewn at the toile/muslin stage

Familiarize yourself with all grain-lines and seam allowances before you sew

Test all interlinings in advance before applying them to a final sample

Remember to select the right needle and thread before you begin sewing

I love to take things that are everyday and comforting and make them into the most luxurious things in the world. **MARC JACOBS**

01

01 — SAMPLE STUDIO
Fashion design sample studios are designed to facilitate the production of first samples. These studios are often supervised and maintained by technical staff to ensure a safe working environment.

The toile

HOW TO USE A TOILE

A toile , or muslin as it is known in the United States, represents the first version of a design transferred into a fabric, such as calico or cotton muslin, to test a pattern. Toiles are used to evaluate an original design and, if necessary, to make alterations or modifications before the first sample is made up in the final fabric. These prototype forms are a work-in-progress but should be approached with care and attention in order to confidently progress towards making up the final design.

Historically, toiles were produced as part of the haute couture system in France. Styles were made for individual clients and wealthy patrons and it was essential to ensure that they fit the client. The toile process allowed the opportunity to review all aspects of the design before cutting up expensive fabrics and investing a great deal of time and skill making up the design. During the 1930s, when many couture houses witnessed a reduction in the number of wealthy clients due to economic downturn, the practice of selling toiles as 'Paris originals' became an established practice among some houses. The revenue from the regulated sale of these toiles became a financial lifeline for some houses and the Paris originals were effectively sold to be reproduced and mass-manufactured. This would later develop into prêt-a-porter, the ready-to-wear industry as we know it today.

Toiles are a practical and cost-effective means of testing and confirming an original design before it is manufactured or made to a client's specification. The process of making a toile provides a valuable opportunity to experiment, explore and evaluate ideas with consideration to practical outcomes. It is always best to apply all finishes, facings and openings to your toile before progressing to the final sample. It is also good practice to draw and mark all your alterations on to the toile so that they can be recorded and transferred to the pattern. More complicated designs or designs that require significant alterations may need to be presented as a second toile. Ultimately, the process of creating a toile should be an assurance that all aspects of the design have been tested and evaluated in the studio. Record and capture the development of a toile in your sketchbooks, either through photographs or observational sketches from a variety of angles. Make sure that you review your toile on the correctly fitting dress stand or review it on a live model. The experience of producing a toile should be rewarding and validate your position as the designer.

GENERAL GUIDELINES AND PRINCIPLES FOR PRODUCING A TOILE/MUSLIN

Toiles can be used to test and confirm a pattern

Toiles should help you to identify and resolve issues relating to fit, cut and shape

Toiles can be used to practise and improve sewing construction, assembly and finishing skills

Toiles should assist with evaluating line, proportion and balance in relation to a design

Creating a toile should inform and confirm the design process

Toile
Toile is a French word that means linen cloth or canvas. Traditionally a linen canvas or calico was used to represent a structured style and a white cotton muslin was used for more fluid or draped styles.

01 — TOILE
Creating a toile/muslin enables a designer to view a prototype from a variety of positions and views. The overall line and balance can then be evaluated and any faults corrected before proceeding to a final sample.
Credit: Laura Helen Searle

01

Fittings and finishings

FIT

EASE

Fit refers to how a garment looks and feels. This is achieved through a combination of factors including cut, shape, fabric, method of manufacture and size. For a toile or final sample to be commercially approved by a fashion designer or a buyer, the garment or outfit should satisfy the fit requirements of the company, with regard to the style of garment target customer and market level.

As previously discussed, the fit of a garment is dependent on a combination of factors. Fit is synonymous with cut, although they are quite distinct from each other. Essentially, a garment may be cut to accentuate the human form or alternatively to add volume or fullness around the body. This will largely be a design decision but has a direct impact on the perception of fit, especially when considered in relation to silhouette and proportion. Balance is another component of fit that should be carefully evaluated during the production of a toile/muslin. As a guide, the right and left side, and front and back of a garment should appear to be even when viewed circumferentially. This does not mean that a garment can't be asymmetrical but rather that side seams should be aligned and hems should be even, where this is appropriate to the design. Poor balance should be corrected by referring back to the pattern or by examining possible sewing irregularities.

Fit is also affected by standard sizing measurements. Two garments with completely different 'fits' might carry the same sizing label. For example, a size 10 blouse would not be expected to have the same fit as a size 10 coat from the same fashion label or collection, since each type of garment requires a fit that is appropriate to its function and takes account of the fabric.

One principle that can be challenging to comprehend in relation to fit is 'ease'. Ease may be understood as the difference between actual body measurements and the measurement of the finished garment. Most garments need to have ease added to accommodate comfort and movement for the wearer. When working from a standard bodice pattern it is easy to forget to add ease, largely because the toile is fitted on an inanimate dress-stand. In reality, all humans need to inhale and exhale as a minimum requirement, which creates movement around the diaphragm. When you factor in additional physical movement such as walking, sitting and lifting, ease becomes an essential requirement for most garments, depending on the choice of fabric. Fabric technologies have seen advances in the development of stretch and bi-stretch fabrics that eliminate the need to add ease. However, woven fabrics will normally require a calculated amount of ease depending on the garment type and intended customer fit.

Ultimately, fit is an essential commercial consideration for all fashion companies: no matter how good a style might look, if it doesn't fit the customer it won't translate into a sale.

01-02 _ FINISHINGS
Finishings on all samples should be considered and appropriately applied to the type of garment and its market level. Finishes serve a variety of practical and decorative functions to enhance a final design.
Credit: Lauren Sanins

01

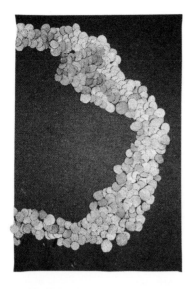

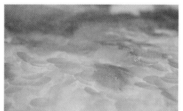

02

silicone sequins
over coated
metallic cotton drill

suede

"waterproof sequins"

coated nylon

silicone sequins
over coated metallic
cotton drill

coated linen

FINISHING

Standards of finish will vary according to the market level of a fashion label and the capabilities of the selected manufacturing unit but will also reflect a company's quality standards. This may involve the production of a sealed sample, where two identical samples are manufactured and agreed in accordance with the fashion company's manufacturing specifications. One sealed sample is held by the manufacturer and the other by the fashion company, with an agreement that there is no deviation from the agreed quality standards during production.

Fashion design students will normally be encouraged to produce a sample to a high set of standards, comparable to a reputable ready-to-wear fashion label, but within the capabilities of the college's design studio. Some students prefer to apply a high standard of hand finishing to a sample garment, which may reflect good taught practices but would need to be adapted for manufacturing purposes if they were commercially produced.

Most fashion students will consider finishes in relation to seams, edges, facings and openings. Each one should be considered on its merits in relation to the garment type, chosen fabric and design.

SEAMS

Illustrated here are the main fashion seams for woven fabrics.

LAPPED SEAM

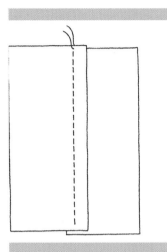

Lapped seam is topstitched and used to eliminate bulk.

If I had an ingenious idea to do fashion that costs less but that wasn't a bad copy of something else... I would do it. With clothes that cost little, you need to ask why they cost so little.

MIUCCIA PRADA

PLAIN SEAM

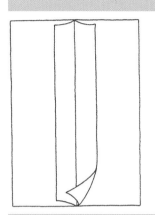

Plain seam is a basic seam where two fabrics are joined together on the right side and pressed open. The edges may be overlocked, depending on the required finish.

WELT SEAM

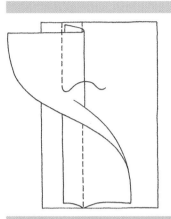

Welt seam is a topstitched seam where one seam is trimmed and enclosed by the other seam allowance. Mainly used on sportswear styles.

FRENCH SEAM

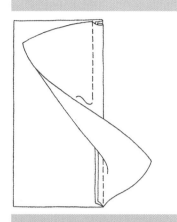

French seam is an encased seam with a clean appearance formed by sewing two fabrics together on the wrong sides before folding, trimming and stitching the right sides together. Suitable for sheer and lightweight fabrics.

SELF-BOUND SEAM

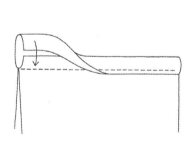

Self-bound seam is sewn as a plain seam with one seam allowance folded over the other and stitched again.

FLAT-FELLED SEAM

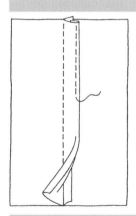

Flat-felled seam is a strong topstitched seam that is stitched on the right side of the fabric and used across a variety of men's casualwear and womenswear.

CURVED SEAMS

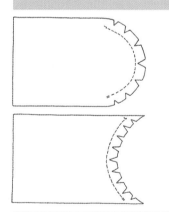

Curved seams are used to join two fabrics along a curved seamline such as a faced neckline or along a curved princess seam. Clipping and notching is required on such seams to accommodate curvature and eliminate excess bulk.

HEMS

Hems are one of the most important edges on a garment and require special attention. All hems should be marked before sewing and can be finished by applying any one of the following:

- Turned-up hem
- Faced hem
- Enclosed hem edge

There are further variations within each category that may be sewn by hand or machine. Decorative finishes can also be applied to hems by topstitching or attaching bindings, piping or cording.

NECKLINES

Most garments require an opening. The type of opening and its position on the garment will usually depend on the design but will have to be considered in relation to its functionality. Many necklines are constructed with facings and combined with an opening feature such as buttons or a zipper. Finishing a neckline on a garment is an important consideration and will usually feature prominently in a design.

Many necklines are joined to collars. Listed below are some of the main necklines and collars to consider as a fashion designer:

- Faced neckline with an interfacing
- Bias-facing neckline
- Piped or corded neckline
- Bound neckline
- Flat collar
- Rolled collar with a stand
- Stand collar
- Shawl collar
- Notched collar and lapel (also known as a rever)

STAND

ROLL LINE

COLLAR OR FACE

BODICE NECKLINE OR GORGE

COLLAR

FALL EDGE OR LEAF EDGE

REVER OR LAPEL

BREAK LINE

CENTRE FRONT BREAK

BUTTON POINT

BUTTON STAND

CENTRE FRONT

01 — COLLAR
Main details for a standard notch collar and rever.

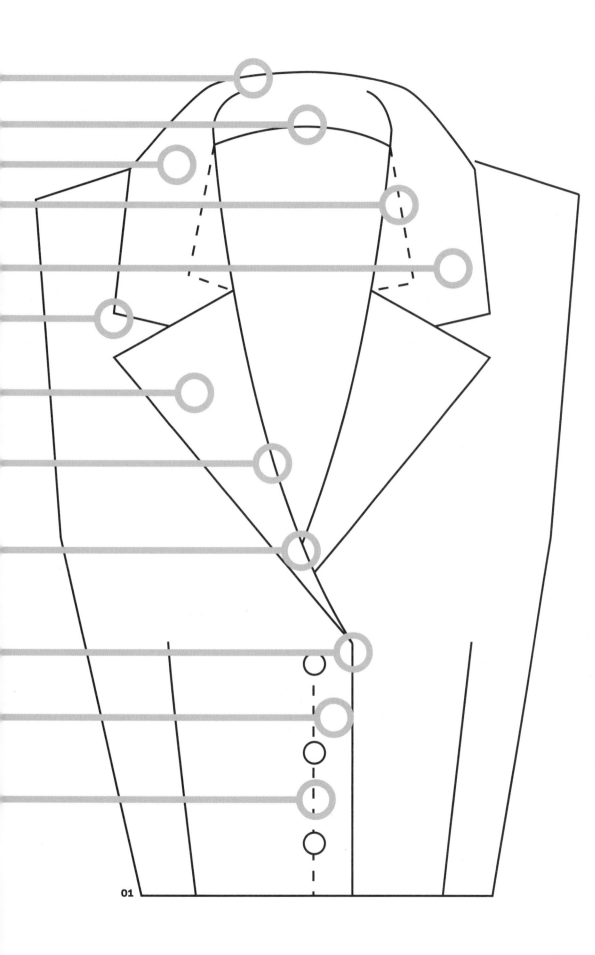

01

The prototype sample

DEVELOPING PROTOTYPES

The prototype sample is the culmination of the design process presented in garment form. Sometimes called a first sample, prototype garments are the outcome of following the design process through the sample room studio from a sketch to a garment.

Fashion design students will be familiar with prototype samples; they are used to progressively challenge and test knowledge, understanding and practical skills by following the critical path from a fashion design concept to the production of a garment or set of garments. A set project or self-initiated brief should provide a creative and commercial context. Practical workshops and technical demonstrations are usually arranged to support projects.

In the fashion industry producing an original sample incurs a series of necessary costs. While a fashion designer will initiate, oversee and present a prototype sample as part of a collection, the decision to include each sample will usually be taken by range coordinators, merchandisers or buyers. Most fashion designers work as part of a team. Many designers are required to present their samples to buyers or range coordinators, who are tasked with making commercial decisions; however, it is the role of the designer and their vision that is central to the production of a first sample.

Approaches to developing prototype samples will vary from company to company. While many ready-to-wear fashion companies use off-shore sources of production for their approved production styles, the critical management process of creating the first prototype sample is often retained in-house. This ensures that the company retains creative control, which can be a critical aspect of its business plan.

For a fashion designer the journey from concept to prototype is a highly personal experience that tests, challenges and consolidates a set of skills and creative decisions towards a defined design outcome. Producing a prototype sample is an integral part of developing a collection.

01 — PROTOTYPE
A prototype sample should confirm a designer's vision having previously been tested for fit and accuracy as a toile. In the industry they are made by a skilled sample machinist. Fashion students will usually be required to make and present their own samples to tutors with supporting development work such as patterns, toiles and sketchbooks.
Credit: Tsolmandakh Munkhuu / Totem

01

Q&A
Maggie Norris

Name

Maggie Norris

Occupation

Fashion designer

Website

www.maggienorriscouture.com

Biography

After graduating from Parsons School of Design in New York, Maggie Norris began her career at Ralph Lauren as creative designer, then becoming senior design director in charge of all women's ready-to-wear and accessory collections. In 1998, Maggie left Ralph Lauren and moved to Europe to work as chief designer for Mondi womenswear. She returned to New York in 2000 to set up her label Maggie Norris Couture. In 2003, she joined the Council of Fashion Designers of America (CFDA).

What motivated you to start your own couture label?

My passion to create couture and the ability to collaborate with other artists and illustrators.

How does heritage and workmanship inspire and influence your work?

Inspiration for me is exploring the classical designs of the past through photography, cinema, music, literature and architecture. As well as bringing inspiration through current contemporary works of art and drawing from what is happening culturally in the world now.

Tell me about your signature corsets

Each of our corsets embodies architectural lines with a sound structure and smooth contours, which accentuate every woman's figure. Once the corset is constructed we appliqué an array of embellishments and archival fabrics for the final couture creation.

What fabrics do you most like to work with and why?

Some of our greatest creations are fabricated with silk duchess satin, silk moiré, 17th century chinoiserie and antique fabrics.

What do you love most about your job?

Knowing that every day I have the ability to collaborate and be inspired by artists and talented craftsmen. Also, enjoying the research process prior to creating new collections, and fulfilling the dreams of clients through our couture.

Tell me about some of your collaborations

We have collaborated with artists such as Anna Kiper, Audrey Schilt, Julie Verhoeven, Bill Rancitelli, Richard Haines, Annie Leibovitz, Mark Seliger, Mert Alas and Marcus Piggott. As well as renowned painter Nelson Shanks, who immortalized our 'Ekatarina' corset worn by Keira Chaplin for her portrait.

What are your plans for the future?

To create and dream!

01—03 _ MAGGIE NORRIS COUTURE

Maggie Norris's custom-made creations have been worn by leading celebrities and socialites including Nicole Kidman, Jennifer Aniston, Sharon Stone and Michelle Obama.
Credit: Maggie Norris Couture

01

02

03

4.0 CONCEPT TO PROTOTYPE

01

01 — BROOKE SHIELDS

Brooke Shields wears the 'Seraphine' corset, fabricated from vintage fabrics and lavishly beaded and embroidered.
Credit: Maggie Norris Couture

02 — ALICIA KEYS

Alicia Keys styled in a 'Sulin Dragon' corset and 'Dragon of the Orient' skirt, created with 18th century chinoiserie, edged with silk hand-tied tassels.
Credit: Maggie Norris Couture

02

Discussion questions
Activities
Further reading

1   Compare and discuss the advantages
    and challenges of creating a pattern
    by using the flat pattern method or by
    draping directly on to a dress stand.

2   Collect a variety of images from fashion
    magazines. Identify individual garments
    and evaluate their cut and fit. Discuss
    the relationship between fit and ease.

3   Collect a variety of woven and knitted
    garments. Identify and compare all
    the seams, stitches, facings and
    finishes. What do they tell you about
    each garment?

1   Use a piece of medium-weight calico
    with the grain-lines marked and apply
    to the centre front of the dress stand.
    Smooth the calico across, keeping the
    weft grain horizontal. Fit around the neck
    and make the shoulder-to-bust dart, then
    the waist-to-bust dart. Trim to fit the
    waistline, complete the side seam. Make
    the back bodice in the same manner.
    Mark up with a fibre-tip pen and trace
    through to create a bodice pattern. Add
    the correct seam allowances.

2   Manipulate the basic bodice block
    to create a princess panel bodice.
    Produce a draft of your style with the
    suppression transferred to the panel
    seams of both front and back. Trace off
    all sections on to new paper and add
    grain-lines, seam allowances and all
    cutting instructions. Make a facing for
    the neckline and armholes.

3   Using the pattern you have created
    for a princess panel bodice, add a flat
    collar. Cut this out as a full bodice in
    medium-weight calico. Join together
    using appropriate seams and overlock
    the edges where necessary.

> The dress must follow the body of a woman, not the body following the shape of the dress.

HUBERT DE GIVENCHY

FURTHER READING

Aldrich, W
Metric Pattern Cutting for Menswear
John Wiley & Sons, 2011

Aldrich, W
Metric Pattern Cutting for Women's Wear
John Wiley & Sons, 2008

Aldrich, W
Pattern Cutting for Women's Tailored Jackets: Classic and Contemporary
John Wiley & Sons, 2001

Amaden-Crawford, C
A Guide to Fashion Sewing
Fairchild Books, 2011

Amaden-Crawford, C
The Art of Fashion Draping
Fairchild Books, 2005

Bray, N and Haggar, A
Dress Pattern Designing
John Wiley & Sons, 2003

Campbell, H
Designing Patterns: A Fresh Approach to Pattern Cutting
Nelson Thornes, 1980

Fischer, A
Basics Fashion Design: Construction
AVA Publishing, 2008

Haggar, A
Pattern Cutting for Lingerie, Beachwear and Leisurewear
John Wiley & Sons, 2004

Homan, G
Bias Cut Dressmaking
Batsford Ltd, 2001

Joseph-Armstrong, H
Patternmaking for Fashion Design
Pearson Education, 2009

Shoben, M and Taylor, P
Grading for the Fashion Industry: The Theory and Practice
LCFS Fashion Media, 2004

Stanley, H
Flat Pattern Cutting and Modelling for Fashion
Nelson Thornes, 1991

The Reader's Digest Complete Guide to Sewing
Reader's Digest, 2010

Ward, J and Shoben, M
Pattern Cutting and Making Up: The Professional Approach
Butterworth-Heinemann, 1987

American Society for Testing and Materials
www.astm.org

Kennett & Lindsel
www.dspace.dial.pipex.com/kennett.lindsell

Siegel & Stockman
www.siegel-stockman.com

Sizemic
www.sizemic.eu

UK National Sizing Survey
www.size.org

Wolf Form Company Inc.
www.wolfform.com

5.0 DEVELOPING A COLLECTION

01

OBJECTIVES

To understand the definition of a collection in the context of fashion design

To identify and appreciate diverse approaches to research for fashion design

To appreciate the purpose and nature of working with sketchbooks

To understand the main functions and processes involved in line planning and range building

To become familiar with costing and pricing definitions and functions relevant to fashion design

To recognize the purpose of reviewing a collection and the role of fashion shows as a presentation format

---

01 — PRESENTING A COLLECTION
Most fashion designers choose to present their collections on models for a catwalk presentation or a lookbook.
Credit: Lisa Galesloot

Defining a collection

RANGE

CAPSULE COLLECTION

In its broadest definition, a collection may be considered as an assortment of garments, accessories or associated products that are linked together in a defined way. They may be linked through a combination of factors such as season, a prevailing silhouette, a complementary or analogous colour scheme, a fabric story or perhaps a specific manufacturing process. The outcome should offer a coherent presentation of ideas translated into designs.

A range or line may be used to describe a more specific grouping of garments or products that are aligned to a commercial sales or marketing plan. This might be a category of garments such as a range of skirts, which would be merchandised across a defined colour palette and fabric story or a group line, which would include items that could be merchandised and sold together as a group. Ranges and lines are interchangeable terms in fashion design. They are also synonymous with the market requirements of the ready-to-wear garment industry.

Fashion design students will be familiar with the term 'capsule collection'. This refers to a collection that is smaller in size than a commercially produced collection but which offers a breadth of designs across different product categories such as skirts, trousers, outerwear, knitwear and tops. Most senior or final-year fashion design students will be expected to prepare a final collection that includes six or more outfits defined by a concept or theme. Capsule collections require the ability to design and edit work into a focused, cohesive offer. They are the culmination of the student's educational experience and require an enhanced level of subject-specific skills in fashion design, including research, sketching, pattern making or draping and the production of final samples. Student collections are usually characterized by personal interests and motivations that might be linked to social, ethical or cultural perspectives.

Chanel is composed of only a few elements: white camellias, quilted bags and Austrian doorman's jackets, pearls, chains, shoes with black toes. I use these elements like notes to play with.

KARL LAGERFELD

01 — CATWALK PRESENTATION
Fashion shows balance artistic spectacle with commercial sales and publicity opportunities. Most designer fashion shows are attended by a mix of buyers, press and front-row celebrities.
Credit: Anne Combaz

EVALUATING A COLLECTION

PRESENTING A COLLECTION

When developing and preparing a collection, all fashion designers are faced with a series of critical decisions that test their abilities and talents. Through the technical processes of pattern making and draping, the designer will be required to evaluate the balance and proportion of a collection. Balance is a very important aspect; it refers to the product assortment and visual 'look' of the collection. It also refers to the relationship between the garments and the designer should consider this when evaluating combinations.

Collections are usually presented to buyers or the press. This may be done privately in-house or presented in an external environment such as a trade event or as part of the annual cycle of fashion shows. Many designer collections include garments that do not make it past the catwalk or runway while other samples are adapted directly from the original to sell to a buyer or account. Collections may also be classified as wholesale or retail collections. This refers to the diverse nature of selling a collection to different sectors of the fashion industry.

01

Research process

While originality and creativity are highly valued and encouraged on most fashion courses, in the industry commercial priorities and economic constraints will influence the approach to research and design. It is important to gain an understanding of how to balance creativity and originality with the needs of the customer or target audience and the realities of working as part of a team.

One of the most important aspects to understand about fashion is its social and collective nature. Fashion does not exist in isolation: it is subject to external influences and perceptual changes in society. Fashion should also be relevant to its position in time and space. Many designers in the industry work as part of a design team. This enables the research process to be part of an interactive exchange of ideas.

For fashion students the equivalent experience will involve discussion with a tutor or professor. The process might include a mind-mapping exercise in a sketchbook to help organize initial thoughts and define one or more directions in which to test and explore ideas. The process of research for fashion design should be systematic and progressive. Establishing a base from which to develop ideas or a sustainable direction can ultimately affect the outcome of a collection's success and appeal. The research process can also be intuitive and emotive. Ultimately, the design process should include a series of steps that help the designer progress from identifying and selecting a direction, theme or concept towards the testing of ideas in the design studio.

Research for design may be understood as either primary or secondary research. Primary research for fashion design refers to original sources or materials that are collected by the designer. It might include, for example, an observational sketch taken during a visit to a museum or perhaps a sketch of a section of a building where the form or shape is directly recorded and later analysed and applied to a design idea for a collar.

Secondary research for fashion design is the use of previously gathered material: published images, text or other data. Secondary sources also include fashion forecasting publications and web-based subscription services that are offered to the fashion industry. Fashion design students will be familiar with college library resources, which are likely to stock a variety of magazines and fashion-related publications.

Most designers use a combination of primary and secondary sources in the development of design research.

01

01 — RESEARCH
Developing a collection involves a period of sustained research. Students are required to provide evidence of the stages of their research and development in order to demonstrate a critical understanding of the processes and outcomes involved.
Credit: Kate Wallis

FABRICS

Undertaking fabric research is hugely important in the context of developing a collection and sourcing fabrics requires care and attention. Fabric stories are developed across all sectors of the fashion industry according to the required lead times of a company. Lead times are dependent upon a company's individual business and operating structure. Designers order sample lengths from which to make a first sample. Most designers will source their fabrics by visiting fabric fairs such as Première Vision. Additionally, many fashion fabrics can be selected and ordered through agents who represent textile mills.

Fashion fabrics vary in price and should be considered in relation to delivery terms and minimum sampling lengths. Ongoing developments in textile production and finishing processes continue to extend fabric choices for designers. Developing a fabric story is an essential part of the design research process and should inspire and support the development of a defined collection.

02 — FABRICS
Designer collections are merchandised into colour and fabric stories that are presented within the format of an overall presentation.
Credit: Anne Combaz

02

COLOUR RESEARCH

Colour can be a source of inspiration but also requires careful consideration as part of a collection plan. Colour inspiration might start from researching natural products, such as examining geological minerals, or by looking at the work of an artist such as Georgia O'Keeffe or Howard Hodgkin.

The application of colour in fashion is linked to seasons and fabric qualities. An understanding of colour theory, as discussed in chapter 3, is an asset, although for some designers the process of working with colour is more intuitive. Fashion designers may work from colour cards presented by mills as part of an open range. Most colour cards are the result of consultation between textile mills and international colour authorities prepared up to two years in advance of the selling season. Designers will usually refer to colour cards or may develop their own colours in consultation with the mills.

Developing a colour story for a collection involves making decisions about how colours interact with each other. Colour blocking is one approach that is used by some fashion designers to emphasize shapes or 'blocks' of colour on a garment or outfit. Accent colours may applied to designs: these are colours that are used to provide emphasis in a scheme. Used sparingly, an accent colour might draw attention to a part of a garment or contribute to the colour rhythm to an overall design. Colour rhythm refers to the interaction between all the colours used in a design.

Patterns provide another element in a colour scheme and can be used to link colours together. Patterns might include printed fabrics, colour wovens or multi-coloured knitted fabrics. The use of patterns or prints can become a defining aspect within a collection; they need to be carefully considered and balanced in relation to the overall colour scheme and proportions of the garments, since pattern requires an understanding of scale and repeat and placement. For some designers the use of pattern and colour is central to their approach.

A viable starting point for commercial designers and fashion students is to visit the stores and identify what is currently available. It is useful to establish an informed view of the market with reference to key looks, fabrics and colours, price points and seasonal items. Many designers seek inspiration from visiting the stores in their home country and overseas as well as seeking out independent boutiques and thrift stores for more unique or individual garments or collections. A designer may buy a contemporary garment or vintage sample from a store to take back to the studio and study in more detail. For designers working in the commercial sector of the fashion industry, store visits are regular point of reference throughout the research process.

01

01 __ FASHION DRAWING
Preparing a fashion illustration allows a designer to convey the look of a collection by communicating colour and texture.
Credit: Kate Wallis

VINTAGE GARMENTS

Vintage garments can offer a breadth of inspiration from which to evolve and develop design research. The distinctive appeal of vintage pieces can be through the cut, fit, shape, fabric or even a trimming or detail on the garment. The best way to approach working with a vintage garment is to respect what it is but to look at how its essence can be translated into a contemporary design.

EXHIBITIONS AND GALLERIES

Exhibitions and permanent collections are a continual source of inspiration for fashion designers. Fashion students are encouraged to visit exhibitions to broaden their cultural outlook, refine their primary research skills, practise their observational drawing skills and work with sketchbooks. World-class museums such as the Victoria and Albert Museum in London and the Metropolitan Museum of Art in New York regularly host special exhibitions in addition to their extensive permanent collections. Smaller museums and regional galleries can also provide valuable resources for fashion designers. Museums hold retrospective shows to celebrate or commemorate the work of fashion designers, such as the Yves Saint Laurent retrospective held at the Petit Palais in Paris or Future Beauty: 30 Years of Japanese Fashion held at London's Barbican. It is useful to study the work of another designer to enhance a critical or intellectual understanding of their work and their design legacy. However, it is not advisable to copy the work of another designer – this is unethical and will only result in a derivative design that does not provide a sustainable approach for developing a collection.

02

02 — DEVELOPMENT BOARD
Research can be a practical experience in the studio environment where a designer tests and explores their ideas as part of the research process.
Credit: Lauren Sanins

FILM, TELEVISION AND MEDIA

Film, television and media have a big influence on fashion and provide the basis for identifying and researching a collection theme. The popularity of *Mad Men*, for example, illustrates how a television series can be picked up and interpreted by some fashion labels into themes for menswear and womenswear collections or styling shoots. Themes are an important component of collections. They offer variety within a collection that can be merchandised into retail looks and delivery consignments.

PHOTOGRAPHY

Photography is closely associated with fashion on many different levels including the photoshoots and lookbooks that many designers prepare and use to communicate their work. Photography exhibitions and styles, both past and present, can challenge and inspire fashion designers by capturing a mood or attitude to inspire a theme or direction for a collection. Photography is a powerful medium, with impact and global reach across digital communication channels and print; it is essential in fashion culture and provides a rich source for visual research.

STREET STYLE

Observing street styles and personal approaches to dressing offers a great source of design research and inspiration. This type of research has expanded in recent years thanks to advances in communication technology and in response to industry demands and corresponding services offered by trend forecasters. Trend spotters, style scouts, photographers and bloggers have all established a presence on the Internet by offering a comprehensive view on style from cities around the world. Additional reportage and photographs of ordinary people in the street, with a sense of personal style, can provide a basis for further research and design development.

01

01 _ VISUAL MEDIA
Fashion's association with film, photography and visual media offer a breadth of research sources and points of reference for fashion designers to draw inspiration.
Credit: Anne Combaz

02 _ STREETSTYLE
Personal style websites, blogs and image-hosting sites may offer additional inspiration and research opportunities to designers.
Credit: Wayne Tippetts / Rex Features

5.0 DEVELOPING A COLLECTION

TRAVEL **ARCHITECTURE**

Travel provides fashion designers with a variety of research opportunities. Visiting another city, country or culture offers a source of inspiration as well as being a culturally enriching experience. Travel also offers fashion designers with the opportunity to undertake market research or competitor analysis. Identifying and understanding cultural and geographical differences is invaluable in preparing collections for export or working with international licensees. Fashion design students are usually offered the opportunity to take study visits at college or university. Such visits may include a combination of arranged cultural activities and market research experiences to retail stores and trade exhibitions, such as Première Vision in Paris.

The style of some fashion designers could be described as architectural. Associations between fashion design and architecture have long been explored by designers over the years and can largely be attributed to interests in analysing shapes, forms and structures. The technical challenges of testing the relationship between the human form and architectural influences can provide a fertile basis for practice-based research in a design studio or a sample room. It is advisable to document technical processes by sketching or photographing studio practice as a work-in-progress. The shape and form of architectural structures also offers a starting point for sketching and testing ideas in the studio through a range of practical processes that include pleating techniques, folding and quilting.

Fashion anticipates, and elegance is a state of mind… a mirror of the time in which we live, a translation of the future, and should never be static.

OLEG CASSINI

01

UTILITY

Utilitarian influences offer another perspective from which to develop a research base for fashion design. This includes analysing and interpreting uniforms, military styles and functional workwear garments and fabrics. Utilitarian themes have become a popular recurring feature across menswear and womenswear collections. The particular appeal of researching military and workwear sources, including denim, is that they offer an opportunity to reinterpret design classics and address functionality and design heritage.

MUSE

Some designers develop themes or entire collections around a muse. In fashion design terms, this refers to a male or female personality, who may be a model or icon, someone past or present, famous or obscure, who in some way inspires or captures a spirit, mood or look. From a research perspective this could involve researching the personal style of a personality, for example Steve McQueen. It then involves working towards an outcome that is likely to be based around forming associations, interpretations and addressing the personality and attitude of the muse in the final garments. Defining a muse can also be combined with other research sources, such as colour research, and offers the intriguing possibility of imagining the muse wearing the final designs.

01 __ WALT DISNEY CONCERT HALL BY FRANK GEHRY
Architecture is a rich source of inspiration. The work of architects such as Frank Gehry may be analysed for form and structure.

02 __ MUSE
Some designers find inspiration from identifying a muse and linking them to the research process. Tilda Swinton has influenced the work and presentations of Dutch designers Viktor & Rolf.
Credit: Catwalking

Working with sketchbooks

DEVELOPING A SKETCHBOOK

WORKING DRAWINGS

Sketchbooks are an essential resource for a fashion designer or a design student. They offer fashion designers the opportunity to record and organize their personal thoughts, motivations and ambitions over a period of time. At their best, sketchbooks should provide an unselfconscious record of a designer's evolving vision and confirm their approach towards a defined outcome or project. In this way, they enable a designer to undertake design research, critical enquiry and investigation so that ideas are explored and tested through a variety of sketches, notes and additional entries. Fashion sketchbooks that have been tightly edited are generally less effective in communicating an idea and lack the freshness and vigour that a sketchbook should offer. At its most fundamental level a sketchbook should present an appropriate selection of sketches. These might include visual analysis of silhouettes, cut, shape, proportion and detailing.

Fashion designers sometimes maintain sketchbooks in conjunction with notebooks, visual diaries, template books and technical files. This approach can work for some designers who prefer to separate collections of fabric swatches and magazine tearsheets or who like to work outside a sketchbook on loose sheets of paper.

Most fashion students will be introduced to sketchbooks as a means of demonstrating their ability to follow the critical path from an initial idea through to design concept. A sketchbook should include working drawings, fabric swatches, observational drawings and photographs of studio practice as it develops. Sketchbooks are usually assessed by tutors or professors as evidence of work in progress and are usually reintroduced for new projects. A sketchbook should offer real insight into the intentions and motivations of a designer as well as their fluency of thought.

Sketchbooks can be used for undertaking primary research: smaller sketchbooks are highly portable and can be used on the go. This makes them ideal for taking to exhibitions and galleries or as part of a visit to the stores to collect and record market research. Larger sketchbooks can offer a designer the opportunity to 'loosen up' by working to a larger format and scale. This can enable experimentation with a variety of colour media as well as encouraging a designer to develop and refine their drawing skills.

In the context of fashion design there is no 'one size fits all' approach to developing a sketchbook. An effective sketchbook is highly personal and diverse. As well as its value in recording and planning a collection, a sketchbook also offers the opportunity for personal reflection, which remains relevant over time and can provide a designer with a personal archive resource.

Working drawings are an important aspect of developing a collection. These drawings are more practical than illustrations or aesthetic drawings and are motivated by the need to problem-solve a garment design or a detail. Working over a previous design to change a collar or pocket is quite usual and reflects a process of refinement through critically analysing previous designs. Working drawing can be a useful lead into producing a draft line-up of a collection. Fabric swatches can be attached and should always be considered as part of a working drawing.

01 __ SKETCHBOOK
Fashion students are encouraged to maintain and update sketchbooks as part of their collection development. Documenting and recording the progress and development of a collection can assist with personal planning and reflection.
Credit: Kate Wallis

01

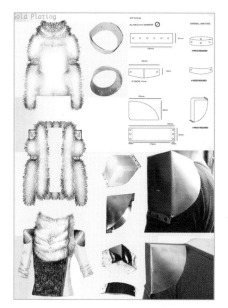

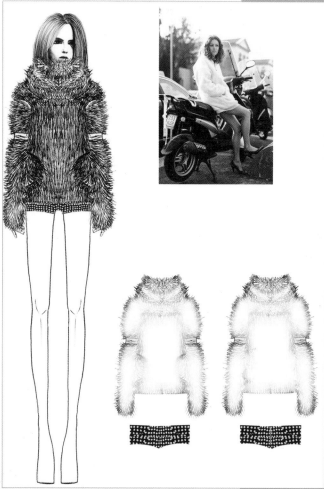

Line planning and range building

SALES REVIEW

FORECASTING

Line planning and range building are important commercial functions in the fashion industry. They are a key function of fashion merchandisers who may consult with designers and buyers depending on the business operating structure of a company. While a fashion designer may set out a design vision for a company, it should be understood as an initial offer that will be subject to input from buyers and merchandisers. Nevertheless, it is important for fashion designers to approach the formulation of a collection with consideration for an intended customer or target market in relation to season, price and product assortment.

In the fashion industry, line planning starts with a review of the previous season's sales by style and product category. Sales trends in the market will be carefully evaluated as part of a team discussion between designers, merchandisers and buyers. The approaches that follow initial planning meetings will vary according to a fashion company's market level and projected business plan. Many companies will review their 'best seller' styles from a previous season and discuss style or fabric modifications with designers. This is sometimes called a 'carry-forward' style. A carry-forward style is usually agreed before any new styles are designed or added to a collection; it is provisionally carried forward as part of a new collection or offered in a different fabric or colourway.

Many ready-to-wear companies will supplement the expertise of their in-house design teams with the services from professional trend forecasting companies such as Peclers, Trend Union, WGSN or Trendstop. The analysis of fashion markets and wider societal influences and trends can help to set a direction for a company's line-planning strategy. Forecasting services are used to identify key elements such as the colour direction for the new season, fabrics and new technologies, key shapes and silhouettes, accessories and suggested themes or looks inspired by haute couture, ready-to-wear designer collections or emerging street styles.

01

MARKET RESEARCH

The fashion design team will usually undertake market research to confirm additional directions and evaluate their market competitors. As previously noted, store visits can be used for inspiration as well as a means of establishing the current market. Preliminary sketches are usually prepared at this time and may be discussed with some buyers or merchandisers if their approval is required later.

SAMPLING

Visits to fabric fairs are useful for identifying suitable fabrics for sampling purposes. Sample lengths are ordered from which to test and create first samples in the sample room, although delivery lead times need to be confirmed as the process of developing a collection is always subject to time constraints and deadlines. The designer will oversee the process of creating a toile or muslin in the sample room. Carry-forward styles may be made up directly into a first sample in a new fabric. The designer will be responsible for reviewing and fitting all samples in the sample room for final approval before they are presented to buyers or merchandisers as part of an in-house presentation or line-planning meeting. The designer will be expected to create a range board, also known as a line sheet. This is a presentation board that visually clarifies a collection proposal by style and fabric. Garments are drawn flat, with front and back views to accurately represent each garment. The primary purpose of a range board is to ensure that the proposed collection offers an appropriate balance and assortment of styles across product categories to fit in with the company's merchandise plan for the season. In addition to designing and creating all the styles that are intended to fit into the merchandise plan, the designer is expected to consider the cost of materials, manufacturing requirements and of course the overall image and market level of the company so that, ultimately, the collection is saleable.

01 — RANGE PLAN BOARD
Range plan boards allow students and designers to visually review and edit their collections. In the fashion industry this function is determined by experienced merchandisers.
Credit: Hanyuan Guo

REVIEW PROCESS

PROJECT BRIEFS

01

Final range planning meetings will include a presentation of the designer's samples made up in fabric with a corresponding range board or line sheet. Prototype samples are usually presented on fit models and will be reviewed for cost, production requirements, merchandise options and overall styling. Most companies will also define and agree a merchandising calendar to include key dates and deadlines for all members of the company to follow. Lookbooks or marketing brochures may sometimes be developed and prepared following the agreement of the final collection. This is comparable to a fashion design student arranging a photoshoot following the completion of their collection.

Fashion design students are usually set project briefs, which are intended to simulate many of the processes already described in developing a collection for presentation. This will typically require a student to formulate a collection through a design process that should be informed by identifying a market or customer for the collection but that also feature a high level of creative investigation and original enquiry. Sketchbook research will contribute to the design development process before designs are translated into a toile or muslin using flat pattern cutting or by draping directly on the stand. Identifying and selecting fabrics is an integral part of developing a collection and defining a fabric story across an assortment of garments. This should translate into a series of balanced outfits where the resulting collection should have an overall look that might be defined by a prevailing silhouette, proportion or colour scheme. Supporting portfolio work might include a series of complementary presentation boards such as a mood board or concept board, flats board or range plan board, line-up sheet and illustration boards.

01—02 _
PRESENTING A COLLECTION
Preparing to present a collection is both an exciting and an anxious time for fashion designers and students.
Credit: Lisa Galesloot

Costing and pricing

Costing and pricing are critical functions that fashion designers should understand and consider in relation to a company's business plan. Fashion design students are also encouraged to acquire a basic understanding of costs and pricing functions and structures. This is usually discussed in relation to costing a garment. Cost refers to the monetary value that is expended to produce a product or service. Price refers to the revenue that is collected from the customer who purchases the product or service. From a fashion design perspective price is also an indicator of quality. As a guiding financial principle, price = cost + profit. Profit refers to the excess of the selling price for the product or service over the cost of producing it.

All commercial fashion businesses need to make a profit in order to sustain their business operations. The role of a fashion designer is to contribute to this critical function. All businesses set their own margins and mark-ups. This is determined by a company's operating structure and business model. Fashion companies operate across all levels of the market from high turnover 'fast fashion' business models to lower turnover designer labels and luxury brands. Turnover refers to the volume of business over a given period of time; it is not the same as profit but is indicative of sales. When the total sales volume generates sufficient revenue to cover all the costs of the business without generating a profit or loss, this is known as the break-even point.

Different costing systems exist across the fashion industry. The primary purpose of costing systems is to track all expenses and incomes over a defined period, usually through quarterly and annual reports, in order to present the company's accounts and establish profit or loss. Listed here are three different costing models that are used in the fashion industry:

- Direct costing calculates all costs that are directly attributed to producing a specific product. These are direct labour costs, material costs and sales commissions as product costs. Other costs such as administrative expenses and overheads are not included.

- Absorption costing includes all direct costs associated with producing a product as the cost base. A pre-determined percentage of some business costs are assigned to product costs while others are included as overheads or operating expenses.

- Activity-based costing (ABC) identifies all activities within an organization and assigns them as constituent elements of product costs. Direct and indirect costs are included and budgeted into product costs. This cost model is widely used in the fashion industry as it facilitates planning, monitoring and control processes, which may fluctuate over a season.

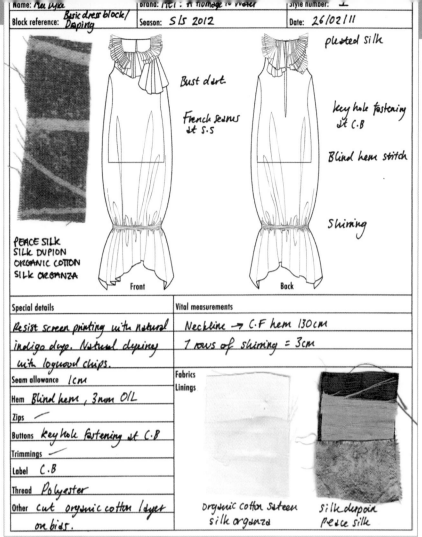

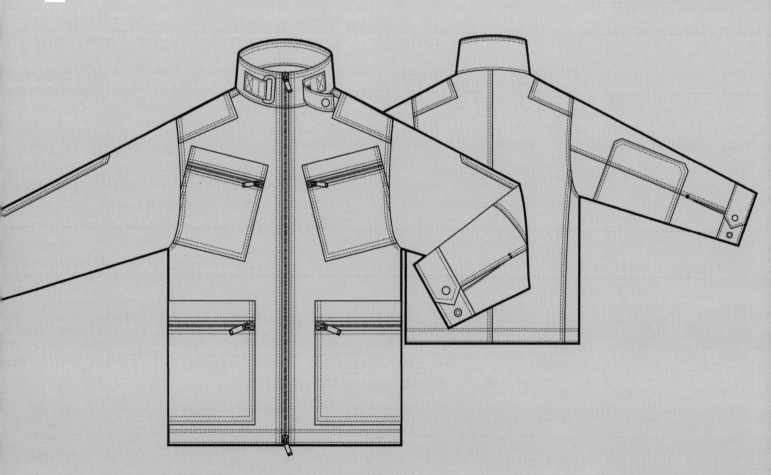

01 — SPEC SHEET
Many fashion students
are encouraged to
prepare specification
and costing sheets for
their final collections.
Credit: Mei Dyke

**02 — TECHNICAL
SHEET**
Understanding
garments is essential
in preparing costings.
Fashion design
students are expected
to produce clear linear
drawings of their
designs.
*Credit: Mayya
Cherepova*

5.0 DEVELOPING A COLLECTION

PROFIT

MARGINS

Establishing a profit or loss position is critical for all businesses. This is determined by understanding the relationship between net sales and the cost of goods sold. Net sales refers to the revenue taken in by a company (gross sales) after all returns and other required adjustments, such as discounts, have been taken into account. In the fashion industry it is not always possible to sell all stock. Sometimes stock is marked down for sale or returned by customers. These adjustments must be calculated into the net sales figure. Once this figure has been established, the cost of goods sold is deducted. Cost of goods sold refers to the inventory costs of goods that are sold over a defined period. This includes direct labour costs, material costs and overhead costs. The cost of goods sold covers fixed and variable costs. Fixed costs remain the same no matter how many units are produced (for example, rental expenses), while variable costs increase or decrease in direct proportion to the number of units produced, such as labour costs or packing and delivery charges.

The difference between net sales and the cost of goods sold is called the gross margin. The gross margin represents the amount that is left over after cost of goods sold is subtracted from net sales. For example, if 65 per cent of a company's net sales have been spent on the cost of producing garments, this would leave a gross margin of 35 per cent. Gross margins are usually expressed as a percentage, called the gross profit margin. To establish a company's net profit or loss, it is necessary to calculate the gross margin and deduct all operating expenses. Operating costs will vary considerably from one fashion business to another and include administrative, advertising and marketing costs. Net profits or losses are subject to taxes but provide the basis upon which to evaluate a business's financial standing. In the context of costing and pricing, fashion design is a cost that is calculated to provide sufficient benefits to a fashion company. It is a critical function within a fashion company's business strategy. Most fashion designers will consider prices in relation to the cost of producing a sample or when reviewing price lists with merchandisers, product development managers or fashion buyers. Designs that are calculated as too expensive or over-priced when fully costed will either be modified, re-costed or removed from a commercial collection.

Fashion design students are usually encouraged or required to prepare costing sheets for their final samples. This offers a useful opportunity to calculate some of the costs associated with producing a finished sample, such as material costs. These include fabrics, linings and all trimmings, such as buttons, zips and threads. Direct labour costs include the cost or cutting, sewing and finishing a garment. They can be calculated by applying a cost value to an hourly rate for each process. Overhead costs are likely to be estimated: these costs will be based on the overheads of the college's sample room, such as the cost of utilities and administration. Costing provides a useful exercise for fashion design students and those who intend to sell their collections after graduation.

01 — GARMENT RAIL
Fashion collections usually comprise of an assortment of garments. In commercial terms, each garment must justify its place in a collection by supporting an appropriate costing and pricing margin.
Credit: Lisa Galesloot

Design is a constant
challenge to balance
comfort with luxe,
the practical with
the desirable. **DONNA KARAN**

01

Presenting a collection

CRITIQUE

The process and format of presenting a collection is an important time for any fashion designer or design student and is charged with a heightened sense of expectation. Essentially, fashion shows are promotional events aimed at encouraging buyers or private clients to place orders and for the press or other media to provide favourable coverage. For fashion design students the prospect of being offered employment is enticing, but it is important to remember that an exciting fashion show does not necessarily equate to a job offer or commercial success. Moreover, fashion shows are expensive events to host, with the ever-present risk of going over budget. That said, it is essential for designers to seek validation for their work and this comes from presenting a collection in a fashion show, lookbook, exhibition and/or a portfolio.

Most fashion design students will be familiar with the practice of presenting their work to their tutors or to visiting designers or industry professionals. These sessions may take the form of a group critique, which provides the student with the opportunity to pause and reflect on their own work and the work of their peers.

While it may be a stressful undertaking for some students, a critique serves many useful functions. To succeed as a designer in the fashion industry one of the most important requirements is the ability to communicate effectively. This includes verbal communication skills as much as the ability to visually present toiles/muslins or prototype samples with supporting work such as sketchbooks or presentation boards. In this way, a critique should be viewed as an opportunity to articulate your ideas in conjunction with presenting samples. Critiques should also be viewed as a forum for exchanging ideas, sharing observations and extending a dialogue that may continue after the critique.

One of the main advantages for students presenting their work to tutors at a critique is the opportunity to receive feedback and advice. The social nature of fashion makes it highly suitable for discussing and receiving feedback as well as an occasion for viewing a garment or outfit on a model or dress stand.

Students are usually encouraged to present prototype samples on live models in order to evaluate their design on a real body that can articulate and move. A critique offers a particularly useful opportunity for evaluating a design proposal when reviewing a collection line-up on models for the first time. If a design appears to work on paper but does not effectively translate into a garment or outfit, the designer should recognize the need to make reasonable adjustments.

Supporting artwork and presentation boards may also be included as part of a presentation or during a critique. These might include a mood board or concept board, flats board or a range plan board as well as a line-up sheet and illustration artwork.

01 __ PLANNING A SHOW
Working with a fashion show producer is an important decision in the preparation and planning of a fashion show. What goes on behind the scenes is critical in making a fashion show look effortless and professional.
Credit: Lisa Galesloot

01

Fashion offers no greater
challenge than finding
what works for night
without looking like you are
wearing a costume. **VERA WANG**

FASHION SHOW PRESENTATIONS

Fashion shows are essentially promotional events. In the fashion industry they are mainly used to present and sell merchandise to an invited audience and to promote the image and standing of a company. Many fashion shows have become high production events and, although some designers continue to explore alternative platforms such as using film or Internet presentations, a catwalk/runway show holds a particular allure. This is also true for many fashion students who view inclusion in a fashion show as a validation of their work. The reality can be different, however, since some collections are less suited to the glare and environment of a live show than others.

All fashion shows require detailed planning, including budgetary considerations and a level of pre-publicity. This includes confirming a venue and agreeing a date, casting and booking models, arranging fittings and preparing a seating plan as well as considering music and lighting requirements. Fashion shows may be in-house events for buyers or agents while other companies will hold them at trade fairs to attract new sales accounts. For fashion students presenting a collection to a prospective employer is usually a strong motivation. Gaining favourable publicity is another motivation that can assist in promoting and identifying a new designer.

Appointing a suitable fashion show producer is an important factor in determining a successful show. Most producers have a wealth of experience and contacts and designers will often form close relationships with their producers, whom they entrust to communicate their vision. Producers can usually assist with selecting models based on the brief from a designer.

Fashion students must usually share models throughout a show and use them in rotation. This make practical and economic sense but can sometimes mean a compromise. While models are important to the presentation of a designer's work and should fit the clothes, ultimately it is the designer's work that will be scrutinized by the trained eyes of the buyers and industry professionals. The best fashion shows look effortless from the front-of-house, which requires efficient management backstage, where models are prepped for hair and make-up and all outfits are arranged for each model in their running order with attendant backstage dressers.

Rehearsals are one of the last stages before a fashion show. Most shows require a rehearsal to include choreography, timing and running order, finale and a light and sound check. At this stage, any errors or timings should be quickly identified and corrected.

Fashion shows are exciting events to be a part of. However, after the lights have gone down, it's important to remember the old fashion adage that 'you're only as good as your last show'.

01—03 _ GRADUATE SHOW
Catwalk presentation of Kate Wallis's graduate collection.
Credit: Catwalking

03

Q&A
Damian Shaw

Name

Damian Shaw

Occupation

Merchandising Director, McQ at Alexander McQueen

Website

www.m-c-q.com

Biography

Damian Shaw began his career as a buyer for Liberty of London. He went on to work as merchandise and marketing director for women's ready-to-wear at fashion house Chloé, where he worked for over six years. After a stint as marketing and merchandising director at Julien Macdonald, Damian began at McQ in 2011.

How did you become a merchandiser?

I started out as a menswear buyer and then moved on to womenswear a few years later. I also bought handbags and small leathers, so by the time I went to work at Chloé I already had a lot of retail and buying experience across most categories of menswear and womenswear.

What's your working relationship with the design and buying teams?

As a merchandiser, you are expected to be the interface between design and commercial. I develop the collection plans in response to the commercial feedback and sales trends and work with the design team to figure out how to integrate the commercial requests into the collection and to ensure that the collection itself is balanced. You have to be the outside perspective; being the watcher.

How has the process of merchandising changed over the years?

The industry has become more merchandising-orientated in general. Everyone is more conscious of what's needed commercially and that it's as important to please the buyers and final customers as to please the press. Otherwise you can find yourself out of business very quickly. The market is so crowded now that the choices you make in terms of design and product strategy have to be really well thought out. The role has become more about merchandising than collection direction, in as much as the role is more pivoted between design and commercial, rather than being about studio management and collection delivery or the interface between senior management of the brand and the creative director. However, I think there's still a difference between how the US sees the role (which is more numbers orientated) and how it works in Europe, where it's more a case of working with design to come up with new product initiatives and to create a commercial framework within which the design process should operate most efficiently.

Talk us through the process of building or editing a collection

The process of building and editing a collection should be understood in the context of working as part of a team. My responsibilities primarily cover collection planning. This means creating the structure for a collection from which the design team work, so it's about providing a framework such as defining number of fabrics, number of styles per category and assessing the overall balance of the collection. Effective merchandising streamlines the design process. It also requires an understanding of the DNA of a brand while looking for commercial opportunities in the market to best represent the creative team's design concept.

What's been the highlight of your career to date?

Every time you get to the end of a season and the collection has sold well and you have the satisfaction of it having worked. Working with talented people, exchanges of ideas, being part of a dynamic team.

What do you love most about your job?

Working with talented people, from both the design and commercial sides of the business. Sharing and developing ideas. Building something successful out of something creative.

01 — MCQ MENSWEAR
McQ by Alexander McQueen SS12.
Credit: Catwalking

5.0 DEVELOPING A COLLECTION

01

02

**01—03 _ MCQ
MENSWEAR**
Merchandisers work closely with buyers as an extended part of the design process to ensure that a collection is viable and ultimately commercial.
Credit: Rex Features / Catwalking

03

5.0 DEVELOPING A COLLECTION

Discussion questions
Activities
Further reading

DISCUSSION QUESTIONS

ACTIVITIES

DISCUSSION QUESTIONS

1 Consider the working processes and critical decisions that are required to design and edit a fashion collection. Discuss these in the context of developing a capsule collection.

2 Discuss the role of research in developing a collection. What constraints or opportunities does it offer a designer?

3 Identify a variety of national and international fashion labels and discuss how their collections are presented and communicated. What does this tell you about the nature and definition of a contemporary fashion collection?

ACTIVITIES

1 Visit a variety of fashion stores to identify the key looks for the current selling season. Consider the colours, fabrics, silhouettes and proportions. Discuss the main influences and directions that are coming through and prepare storyboards to propose new themes that you believe will be relevant or directional for the following season.

2 Prepare a merchandise plan for your collection by identifying and presenting flat drawings for all garments with fabric swatches. Evaluate the overall balance and assortment of your collection. Look at how you could optimize the offer to a retail customer by merchandising the collection across a variety of fabrics and colourways.

3 Identify all your material costs and prepare a costing sheet for each garment in your collection. Calculate a selling price to cover your additional direct labour costs and overheads and add your profit margin. Prepare an invoice for all the garments or outfits to be sold.

FURTHER READING

> Good design is making something intelligible and memorable. Great design is making something memorable and meaningful. **DIETER RAMS**

Carr, H
Fashion Design and Product Development
John Wiley & Sons, 1992

Davies, H
100 New Fashion Designers
Laurence King, 2008

Davies, H
Fashion Designers Sketchbooks
Laurence King, 2010

Faerm, S
Fashion Design Course: Principles, Practice and Techniques: The Ultimate Guide for Aspiring Fashion Designers
Thames & Hudson, 2010

Fukai, A and English, B
The Cutting Edge: Fashion from Japan
Powerhouse Museum
(illustrated ed), 2005

Hopkins, J
Basics Fashion Design: Menswear
AVA Publishing, 2011

Jenkyn Jones, S
Fashion Design
Laurence King, 2011

McAssey, J and Buckley, C
Basics Fashion Design: Styling
AVA Publishing, 2011

Nakamichi, T
Pattern Magic
Laurence King, 2010

Nakamichi, T
Pattern Magic 2
Laurence King, 2011

Renfrew, E and Renfrew, C
Basics Fashion Design: Developing a Collection
AVA Publishing, 2009

Seivewright, S
Basics Fashion Design: Research and Design
AVA Publishing, 2007

Sissons, J
Basics Fashion Design: Knitwear
AVA Publishing, 2010

Udale, J
Basics Fashion Design: Textiles and Fashion
AVA Publishing, 2008

Lectra
www.lectra.com

Peclers Paris
www.peclersparis.com

Trendstop
www.trendstop.com

WGSN
www.wgsn.com

Signe Chanel - Haute Couture Collection
DVD, 2008

Vivienne Westwood - Art Lives
DVD, 2009

Yves Saint Laurent
DVD, 2007

6.0 PORTFOLIO AND PROFESSIONAL PRACTICE

———

OBJECTIVES

———

To understand the purpose and value of a fashion design portfolio

To identify a range of opportunities for self-promotion as a fashion designer

To consider the impact of information communication technology on the fashion industry

To appreciate the variety of career paths associated with fashion design

To gain an enhanced understanding of job roles and their inter-relationships within the fashion design sector

To encourage further reading in preparation for a career in fashion design

———

01 — RODARTE INSTALLATION
Pale pink and bright pink silk georgette and silk chiffon pleated and draped gown, with hand-beaded Swarovski crystal elements, tassels with gold pleated metal and ray breast plate. *Credit: gown by Rodarte, photograph by Autumn de Wilde, installation by Alexander de Betak at Pitti Immagine W in Florence, Italy*

01

6.0 PORTFOLIO AND PROFESSIONAL PRACTICE

Fashion portfolios

DEVELOPING A PORTFOLIO

A fashion portfolio is a body of work that communicates your design ideas and presentation skills across a range of visual formats. It should also indicate your creative abilities, personal strengths and subject interests, for example womenswear or menswear. Portfolios may be presented within a physical portfolio case or in a digital format. Those in portable cases – usually in A3 or A4 – enable the presentation of tactile fabric swatches and textures, which enhances the experience for those reviewing the work. Digital portfolios, also called e-portfolios, can be useful for backing up work or preparing artwork for presentation on a blog, website or image-hosting site.

A3 A4
A3 and A4 are paper sizes within the widespread international ISO standard, while North America follows a different system.
A3 = 11.7 x 16.5in
A4 = 8.3 x 11.7in

Most fashion design students are expected to produce a physical portfolio of presentation artwork. This becomes an evolving process of collecting and documenting work over a period of time to display a suitable diversity of projects. Although each student will be very familiar with their own projects it is important to understand that all work in a portfolio needs to be communicated directly to a viewer without unnecessary over-description during an interview. This requires a process of critical evaluation, selection and editing in order to coherently communicate each project, and justify its inclusion within the portfolio, to someone who is unfamiliar with the work. A fashion design portfolio should evolve but remain relevant to your experiences and interests.

A fashion design portfolio provides a designer with the opportunity to make a good first impression. As such it should show what you do best and represent you in the best possible way. This is achieved by organizing the content into an appropriate sequence of work and considering the central purpose of a portfolio as a self-promotion and sales tool. There is little value in padding out a portfolio with substandard work or repetitive presentations and ideas, which can be counter-productive.

Although there is no such thing as a 'one size fits all' approach to formulating a successful fashion design portfolio, listed here are some areas of good practice that should assist in preparation.

Ultimately your portfolio should be tailored to your intended career path in the fashion industry or to the requirements of a company when preparing for an interview. Fashion design portfolios should be technically and artistically competent. The overall content and presentation of all artwork should be arranged in a way that all projects remain visually appealing and appropriately sequenced while reflecting a consistently high standard. Striking a balance between offering sufficient breadth and quality is a key determinant in establishing a successful fashion design portfolio.

Whether you are preparing a physical or digital portfolio it is worth remembering that for a fashion designer, your portfolio should represent the visual centrepiece of your personal promotion.

DO

Make sure that your artwork will fit into the sleeves of your portfolio case.

Ensure that all the sleeves in your portfolio are spotlessly clean. Good artwork will quickly lose its appeal if the sleeve is marked or dirty.

Open your portfolio with some of your best work to create a positive first impression.

Edit and review your work to ensure that the content and organization is appropriate to your presentation or interview requirements.

Consider the position of artwork on facing pages when the sleeves are spread open.

Use a variety of presentation formats in your portfolio to add visual interest but be consistent within each project.

Make sure that all titles and letters are clear and legible where they are used on boards.

Ensure that all fabric swatches are neatly trimmed and mounted.

Make sure that all digital images and print-outs are correctly pixelated.

Ensure that you use an appropriate adhesive when mounting artwork to avoid creating unsightly air pockets.

Be prepared to discuss your portfolio if you have to present it, but be concise.

DON'T

Don't include unnecessary work in your portfolio just to add content. This could make you appear indecisive or desperate.

Don't mix landscape and portrait format within the same project.

Don't make excuses or apologize about your work. If you aren't confident to present it then don't include it in your portfolio.

Avoid artwork with raised surfaces or fold-out presentations. They are not suitable for insertion within a portfolio sleeve.

Avoid isolated boards that don't relate to projects as they will appear out of place or distract the viewer.

Avoid the use of prominent dates on artwork as this may work against you after a few seasons.

Don't try to present yourself as a designer for all markets and occasions. Your portfolio should reflect a market orientation.

Avoid repetition through your designs or presentation formats.

Personal promotion

DIGITAL PORTFOLIOS

BLOGS

During the past decade, many aspects of the fashion industry have been transformed through rapid advances in communication technology and the rise of social media. Fashion designers are not immune to such changes. Fashion design students are increasingly expected to embrace new media technologies as a means of marketing their skills, building contacts and securing a competitive advantage in a diverse international market.

Digital portfolios, also called e-portfolios, are used by fashion designers to back up their work as a portable digital file or to provide an alternative presentation format to a client or during an interview. They are an efficient means of presenting image and text-based work. Additionally, technology such as motion graphics or interactive links can be embedded in an e-portfolio presentation. Digital portfolios also offer the opportunity to combine scanned artwork with photography, such as artwork and a photoshoot for a collection lookbook. Preparing a digital portfolio enables a fashion designer to upload their work across a variety of web-based applications including blogs and websites.

Ever since web-logs, known as blogs, appeared in the 1990s, their impact and potential has grown and been developed by individuals and corporate brands alike and used to communicate directly with a potential global audience. Thanks to low overheads and user-generated content, blogs are an accessible platform for fashion design students to post their work and communicate directly to site visitors. Fashion blogs have become an established part of the fashion communication industry, and these days the more established bloggers sit on the front row at the shows with members of the fashion media. Blogs are relatively easy to set up, with a number of host providers including Blogger, Word Press and Tumblr all offering ready-made templates. Depending on the hosting service, scanned images, photographs, text, hyperlinks, audio, video and slide shows can all be embedded and customized within a blog.

01

01 _ ISSUU
The growing impact and influence of image-hosting websites and digital publishing platforms has enabled fashion students to post their portfolios online. Detail from a digital portfolio by fashion graduate Sophie Davison at www.issuu.com

WEBSITES

The Internet features a huge variety of fashion-orientated websites, so getting noticed requires selectivity and marketing prowess. In addition to website services that may be offered by education institutions to promote the work of students and alumni, you may consider setting up your own website. This will involve registering a domain name with a reputable hosting service and generating web space to suit your anticipated needs. At its most basic level a website can serve as a personal homepage; it might be linked to a blog that is regularly updated. However, the potential of a website is far reaching in terms of showcasing a business profile or marketing interface. Making a website navigable and easy to use is crucial.

A good alternative is to join a hosting website. The Arts Thread site, for example, allows fashion design students and graduates in other creative disciplines to upload their portfolios and has searchable functions for prospective employers to browse. Coroflot also offers a range of services to registered users including searchable e-portfolios. The site is used by a wide range of international business clients who scan it regularly to identify potential talent.

IMAGE-HOSTING SITES

Image-hosting websites have gained a significant presence on the Internet. Their visual interface makes them highly suitable for fashion design students and others working with visual media or photo sets. Some of the most established sites, including Flickr, Carbonmade and Lookbook, enable members to store, manage and organize images and online portfolios. Image-hosting sites are similar to social network sites, with the option to contact the user, view a user's profile or search for professional contacts or prospective employers. The growth and popularity of such websites is indicative of their potential to combine self-promotion and networking opportunities with flexible access.

It is a company's customers who effectively control what it can and cannot do.

CLAYTON M. CHRISTENSEN

SOCIAL NETWORKING SITES

STUDENT EXHIBITIONS

Social networking sites offer fashion designers and students further opportunities to create profiles and develop extended networks. One such example is Facebook, which launched in 2004 and has since become a dominant force in the United States and around the world. This has enabled Facebook to leverage its considerable marketing capabilities and attract corporate names to sign up to the site as a means of communicating with new or established customers.

Launched as a business-orientated social network site, LinkedIn offers fashion designers and graduates the opportunity to make professional contacts. It also enables prospective employers to review profiles and identify business opportunities through a contact network.

Fashion design students will usually be offered an end-of-year exhibition at their college or university (known as a senior show in the United States). These exhibitions represent work from each student in the form of portfolio, sketchbooks and completed garments. The exhibitions are organized and financially supported by the host college and intended to offer a platform to graduating students while also promoting a collective view of work undertaken during the final year of study. One of the most important aspects of these shows is the public access: industry professionals may be invited to view the work on display. Sometimes an accompanying fashion show may be arranged with a live weblink and a homepage to profile participating students. In addition to the college exhibitions an external exhibition may also be arranged as part of an organized event such as Graduate Fashion Week in London.

02

01

01 — ARTS THREAD
Arts Thread is a dedicated creative graduate website that links education with industry contacts. Students can upload their portfolios to the Arts Thread media site with flexible search functions and links.

02 — PRESENTING PORTFOLIOS
Portfolios are an essential personal promotion and marketing tool for creative graduates, including fashion design students.

INDUSTRY EXPERIENCE

Internships and work experience can provide a valuable learning opportunity for fashion design students to supplement their taught programme of study. Internships, also called work placements, are often an arrangement between a college and an employer. The arrangement is formally recognized and agreed in accordance with the obligations of both parties and regulated by the education institution. The employer will usually provide a report or reference upon completion to enable the college to award course credits. Such arrangements are formally embedded into some courses and may extend over the overall duration of study.

Work experience is informally arranged and does not count towards course credits. It is usually undertaken outside term time and does not extend the duration of study for the student. Work experience is also a valuable learning opportunity; it may be facilitated by course instructors or self-initiated by the student.

All forms of work experience provide excellent opportunities for networking and developing professional contacts. For most students they also offer a real introduction to a working environment within the fashion industry. Personal experiences can vary considerably so the student and employer expectations should be realistic. Many employers recognize the learning and training benefits provided by the work experience and therefore may not offer payment. From the employer's perspective, the student will leave with experiences that can benefit a future employer so the knowledge and skills gained may be thought of as a payment in kind. Additionally, most fashion students will list their work experiences on their CV or resumé. This can add value to an application and generate interest when applying for a job. Ultimately, all work experience opportunities offer benefits to a fashion student and can help focus their interests and identify their strengths as they prepare for a career in the fashion industry.

01

01 — INTERNSHIPS
Internships offer students valuable work experience opportunities and often count towards course credit.
Credit: Nils Jorgensen / Rex Features

Career opportunities THE DESIGNER

The fashion industry is a diverse global employer, offering a range of job roles and career opportunities for talented and ambitious graduates. The professional opportunities open to design graduates include a variety of creative, technical and retail positions across the fashion industry. It is important to remember that whatever job you perform in the fashion industry you will be required to work as part of a team or contribute to a team structure: interpersonal skills are essential and highly valued across the sector.

Fashion designers are essentially responsible for providing a creative direction to a fashion label or brand with contemporary and commercial relevance. Working as part of a team, the designer is involved in leading or contributing to the collective vision of a label by realizing and sometimes promoting a new collection or line. The individual role and job requirements of a designer will vary depending upon the level of responsibility and the business and operating structure of the company. Described here are the main categories for employment as a fashion designer, with additional career paths that are also applicable to fashion graduates according to individual interests and skills.

A fashion designer works as part of an extended team that usually includes a pattern cutter, sample machinist and garment technologist, as well as buyers and merchandisers. The process of formulating a new design initiates a sequence of activities that involves other people. Some companies employ large teams of designers; smaller companies may only employ one or maintain a small, cohesive team. Either way, the critical path from design inception to final sample is followed through a series of defined stages that link research activities with internal presentations and review meetings or external presentations such as fashion shows.

Traditionally, most fashion companies produce seasonal collections based on a recurring annual cycle of selling seasons from spring/summer to autumn/winter. Now, however, advances in communication technology, more efficient supply-chain management systems and the effects of globalization have all given rise to inter-seasonal collections and pre-collections that are presented to buyers to meet strict commercial deadlines.

Pre-collections are in-between lines that are designed and delivered to stores ahead of the mainline designer collections in January and June. They are developed with buyers ahead of the selling season to offer wearable and affordable lines; they are not presented as part of the biannual fashion week catwalk presentations. Pre-collections include clothing and accessories that work across the seasons and they have become an important commercial aspect of the fashion industry and the designer-buyer relationship. For fashion students the term pre-collection is synonymous with preparing and testing ideas for their final graduating collections.

The process and cycle of designing a new collection will depend on a company's business model. Some companies produce wholesale collections; others produce retail-only, private label collections, which are only sold through their own stores. Vertically structured and international companies may produce wholesale and export collections in addition to retail-only or limited-edition collections. Designers may also work for companies that produce collections under licence or work for a manufacturer-supplier to a private label. The role of a designer within each business model will vary considerably depending on the company's business objectives and view of design.

01 — VIVIENNE WESTWOOD
Fashion designer Vivienne Westwood in her studio. Many designers create inspiration walls in their studios, where the design team can contribute visual ideas.
Credit: Philip Hollis / Rex Features

01

6.0 PORTFOLIO AND PROFESSIONAL PRACTICE

WOMENSWEAR DESIGNER

Many designers working in the fashion industry today are associated with womenswear. This reflects the retail diversity of the sector, which spans a variety of product categories.

Most womenswear designers are usually required to produce a series of presentation boards, to include a colour palette. Colour palettes tend to be linked to visual sources of inspiration that are defined by themes or trends. Meetings may be held with buyers to confirm or refine the colours before they are submitted to suppliers for lab-dips or to match to colour cards from textile mills. Most designers will produce mood boards to establish the tone and visual context for a new collection or line and a direction for design development that best reflects the design label or brand image.

As discussed in chapter 5, the designer undertakes a research process for design, considering a variety of influences and inspirations in order to formulate a series of sketches or working drawings. This could include examining vintage garments, street styles, film or media influences, travel, architecture, the work of an artist or any inspiring exhibition. Attending trade exhibitions and visits to the stores will usually inform the sketching process. Some designers produce inspiration walls in their studios where the design team all contribute visual ideas. These are discussed and the designing is shared or allocated across the team.

A process of editing and refining design ideas will follow as the designs are arranged into a visual range plan or line sheet. Internal presentations to the senior designer or buyers are then scheduled to confirm and agree styles that will be developed into samples in the sample room.

The designer will visit the sample room to submit and review the prototype samples with the pattern cutters throughout the design cycle. This may be done in-house or through an out-house or overseas sampling unit. Reviewing and fitting all samples is a critical responsibility that is managed between the designer and pattern cutter. As part of the process of sampling, costings are prepared so that when samples are presented for internal presentations and fit meetings with buyers, merchandisers and garment technologists, the designs can be assessed for their suitability and inclusion in a collection or line. For fashion design students, many of these functions are simulated during the process of preparing a final or senior collection.

MENSWEAR DESIGNER

Working as a menswear designer encompasses many of the functions and processes involved for womenswear, with particular consideration to technical skills and manufacturing processes. Colours and fabrics are researched in the context of the different product categories across the menswear sector. These include casual and sportswear lines, including active sportswear, to more classic, functional styles including suits and formal tailoring. The menswear sector operates on many different market levels, spanning branded streetwear to more formal, traditional styles.

Dedicated menswear trade fairs and exhibitions are visited by designers and buyers to confirm seasonal directions and emerging influences. Menswear designers also work with sketchbooks and produce a variety of presentation boards as part of the design process, presenting themes and inspiration, colours and fabric trends as well as range plans or line sheets. Producing technical drawings is an important aspect of working as a menswear designer in the sportswear sector. This will require CAD skills for vector and bitmap software. There are many freelance design opportunities available to menswear designers within the sportswear sector. For those working in the more formal sectors, including tailoring, it is essential to have good technical design skills in order to be able to effectively evaluate cut and fit and to work effectively with a menswear cutter or tailor.

KNITWEAR DESIGNER

Working as a knitwear designer combines creativity with subject-specific technical skills. Individual job roles will vary according to a company's manufacturing techniques. Machine knitting may be broadly divided between fully fashioned knitwear and cut-and-sew knitwear. Fully fashioned knitwear is shaped as it is being knitted. This is more expensive to produce and as such, fully fashioned techniques are less applicable to commercial production. Cut-and-sew knits are produced from a length of knitted fabric that is cut to shape and sewn together. This method is more widely used in the industry. Hand knitting offers a distinctive alternative to the machine knitting process but is less applicable to commercial production.

Knitwear designers follow a research process much like woven designers; however, they must select yarns with particular attention to colour and texture since they also create their fabric as part of the design process. It is essential to have the necessary technical skills to work as a knitwear designer. These include an understanding of tensions and gauges, and how to knit across a variety of industry standard knitting machines, working with single- and double-bed carriages.

Knitwear designers also work with sketchbooks and are required to develop presentation boards and specification sheets for manufacture. An awareness of fashion trends and market requirements is important for knitwear design, combined with the technical knowledge to create fabric structures and textures.

01

01 — KNITWEAR DESIGN
Dress by knitwear designer Craig Lawrence, incorporating unconventional materials to create volume, texture and lightness.
Credit: Totem

PATTERN CUTTER

Pattern cutting is a technical skill that requires detailed knowledge of garment construction in order to translate a design into a credible prototype garment. Most pattern cutters work closely with designers to interpret a design from a sketch or working drawing. In some cases the pattern cutter and designer form a close working relationship, where both parties intuitively understand one another and the pattern cutter can work directly from a design sketch to produce a toile/muslin. The pattern cutter works alongside the sample cutter and machinist and is required to communicate with garment technologists and designers before a sealed sample can be approved.

All design companies hold a catalogued archive of their sample patterns across a range of styles, providing a valuable record of the different fits and shapes that have been produced over the years. Some pattern cutters and designers will start by reviewing a pattern from a previous season as the basis for updating or modifying a style for a new collection. This approach is quite common in the ready-to-wear fashion industry and is associated with product development as much as design creation.

Many fashion design companies invest in a sample room for in-house pattern cutters to produce original sample patterns in conjunction with the designers. Others pay professional freelance pattern cutters to produce sample patterns. This may involve supplying the pattern cutter with a specification sheet and guidance on measurements or a garment to use as the basis for producing a pattern. Sometimes a competitor sample may be sent to a pattern cutter to copy. Although it does not represent good industry practice, commercial imperatives have encouraged some firms to follow this route. Other companies delegate the process of pattern cutting to a factory unit to produce a fully factored or 'bought-in' sample at an agreed price. This has become established practice for companies that work with reliable off-shore manufacturers.

Fashion design students are introduced to pattern cutting on most design courses and will produce patterns as part of the process of creating a prototype sample or preparing a collection. Those who aspire to work as pattern cutters in the fashion industry will need to gain practical experience and be able to work to deadlines. Pattern cutters usually start out as a trainee or junior pattern cutter and progress on to senior pattern cutter or sample room manager depending on experience and expertise.

SAMPLE CUTTER

Sample cutters work in the sample room as part of a technical design team, working closely with the pattern cutter. The sample cutter is responsible for laying out the sample length of fabric before cutting it out with shears. This requires a steady hand and close attention to detail and accuracy to maintain a straight grain and selvedge. The sample cutter is also responsible for arranging the most economical lay plan for each style; some fabrics can only be cut one way. As part of this process the sample cutter will make a record of the lay plan and provides a preliminary costing based on the quantity of fabric used. This information is added to the specification sheet and pattern envelope. The sample cutter marks out the pattern pieces on the fabric, which is held down with weights, and then makes an accurate cut out including notches. Lining patterns are also cut out, along with any fusible pieces such as interlinings, which are used to stabilize or reinforce fabrics. When all the fabric, lining and fusible pattern pieces have been cut out they are rolled into a bundle and tied with a spare length of fabric. The designer's drawing, the patterns and any trimmings such as zips or buttons are attached to the bundle of cut work, which is now ready to pass to the sample machinist.

01 — PATTERNS
Patterns for making first samples are usually prepared in cardstock before being numbered and archived to enable the pattern cutter and designer to refer to them in the future. Over time this can become a valuable resource and provides a record of evolving styles and fits.
Credit: Ray Tang / Rex Features

02 — SAMPLE CUTTING
Sample cutters are skilled professional who are primarily responsible for cutting out the first sample and working closely with a sample machinist to produce a prototype sample for the designer.

01

02

GARMENT TECHNOLOGIST

The garment technologist is the critical link between the designer, the pre-production sample and the finished garment. They work in association with designers, pattern cutters, factories and production staff to agree and maintain quality standards and fitting requirements, monitoring the production process and checking for any faults on the garment or fabric as part of a rigorous process of quality control. In many companies a first sample is sent to a factory or CMT (cut, make and trim) unit to confirm costings and assess suitability for manufacture before a commitment to production can be agreed.

The sample is manufactured according to the design specification sheet and submitted to the design company for a fit meeting. This requires the sample to be worn by a fit model who conforms to the company's size scale for a sample. Such meetings are attended by the designer, and often a buyer, to review and agree any alterations with the garment technologist, who makes detailed notes for the manufacturing unit to follow precisely. No deviations are accepted from the sealed sample. Sealing refers to the process of finalizing all necessary requirements for the manufacture of a sample; this serves as a control measure and becomes a contract between the design company and the manufacturer. The garment technologist checks the results of any fabric tests, such as for colour fastness or shading. Finally, a graded size chart is prepared and sent to the manufacturer to start production.

The garment technologist is required to inspect the production sample and accept or reject it (rejecting a style will usually be based on a deviation from the sealed sample), as well as address and resolve technical problems that may arise during manufacturing. Garment technologists need to be well-organized, have an eye for detail and possess good computer literacy skills in order to prepare spreadsheets and technical data.

PATTERN GRADER

Pattern grading is a specialized technical discipline for sizing patterns up or down to a specified scale. A pattern grader will follow a prescribed system of applying mathematical gradients and ratios to pattern pieces to size them up or down. It is important to have an understanding of body shapes in order to understand the principles of grading, since not all sides of the pattern are graded. The resulting set of patterns is called a nest of grades. Individual sizes vary according to the company's sizing system; it may cover numeric sizes or an S, M, L size scale. Traditionally produced by hand, grading has now become a digitized process, requiring professional pattern graders to work with specialized software such as Lectra Modaris, TUKA and Cadassyst. Accuracy and attention to detail are essential requirements for a pattern grader. Educational software is available on some fashion/clothing technology courses. It is also possible for technically minded individuals to enter the industry through apprenticeships.

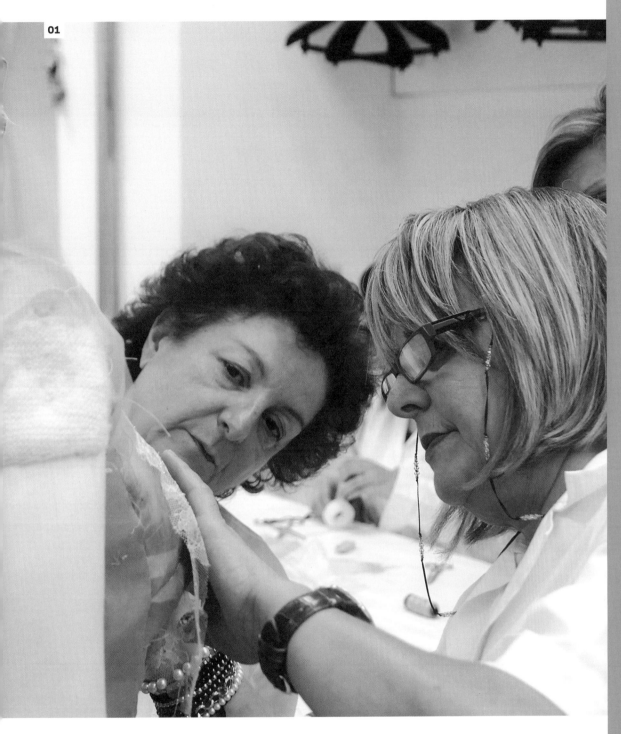

01

**01 — GARMENT
TECHNOLOGISTS**
The process of
preparing and sealing
a sample will involve
the critical eye and
analytical skills of a
garment technologist
working in a technical
team. A sample may
undergo any number of
modifications before
it can be approved for
production.
*Credit: AGF s.r.l. / Rex
Features*

I like to dress egos.

GIANNI VERSACE

FASHION BUYER

Fashion buyers work across all sectors of the retail fashion industry as part of a buying team. The buyers are responsible for preparing a merchandise buying plan ahead of the selling season. This might involve the **open to buy (OTB)** model for fashion buying or assortment planning and will largely depend upon the size and structure of each business organization and the target market. Fashion buyers are primarily responsible for raising contracts with suppliers and placing orders. Consequently they need to be able to identify and compare suppliers in order to negotiate terms. This may involve attending trade fairs and exhibitions, which may introduce them to the work of new designers. Buyers are also responsible for accepting and raising payment for ordered goods and services. This may involve placing orders with manufacturers, wholesalers, agents, importers or even other retailers, depending on the nature of the business.

Open to buy (OTB)
Merchandise that is budgeted for purchase during a certain time period but has not yet been ordered. It is also the process of planning merchandise sales and purchases.

Always working within a budget, a fashion buyer will negotiate on price, including discount terms for prompt payment, and terms of delivery. A good buyer is able to recognize quality and service when assessing the most suitable type of merchandise for their retail space. The selection of merchandise is critical and should reflect the image of the company. This usually involves presentations and meetings with the design team. Companies that operate a wholesale and retail business will schedule regular meetings between in-house design teams and their buyers. These meetings provide necessary dialogue between the designers and buyers, where the buyers offer valuable feedback on lines that are selling while the design team may present and propose new ideas and directions. In some companies, the buyers work closely with designers as part of the sampling process and may travel overseas with the designers to meet suppliers or to visit factories to source new products.

Independent fashion designers without their own retail outlets must present their ranges to buyers who may represent a department store or an independent boutique. This type of presentation to a buyer requires detailed planning and should be conducted professionally if an order is to be secured. Meeting deadlines is essential.

All buyers work to critical schedules, which includes dates for ordering and receiving approved samples. Additionally, they must manage their budgets and work with merchandisers to confirm size ranges and allocations to the stores. Fashion buyers usually start out in junior buying roles. They should be able to combine commercial flair with financial acumen and have a solid understanding of fashion products and market trends.

01

01 — FASHION BUYING
Fashion buyers often buy from wholesale collections that are presented at national and international trade shows and exhibitions.
Credit:
breadandbutter.com

MERCHANDISER

Merchandising can be defined as the planning involved in providing the right merchandise in the right place, at the right time, in the right quantities and at the right price. This concise summary, adapted from the American Marketing Association's definition, offers an insight into the critical business function of fashion merchandising and its inter-relationship with the design and buying processes. Fashion merchandisers work closely with buyers and garment technologists to produce a merchandise plan. This sets out the company's financial commitment to invest in a line or collection, with consideration for product assortment by colour, fabric and sizes, against agreed delivery dates to a distribution warehouse. Once each production sample has been approved by the senior garment technologist, a merchandiser may issue a manufacturer's delivery approval note to enable delivery to a warehouse and distribution to stores. The supply chain process requires detailed management. Sometimes members of the quality control team at the warehouse will check samples before allowing the driver to dispatch items to stores and will report back to the garment technologist and merchandiser if there is a problem.

The merchandise team includes allocators, who act as the interface between the merchandise plan and stock distribution. They are responsible for allocating and replenishing stock where it is needed, to ensure that each store has the optimal assortment of merchandise in order to maximize potential sales and profit revenues. What might sell in one location may not sell in another, so regional differences may need to be considered as well as local competition. Allocators may also offer recommendations to buyers about distribution, which is informed by their detailed knowledge of inventory levels.

Merchandisers monitor sales figures on a daily or weekly basis and report these to the merchandise director. Many large fashion organizations employ merchandise analysts who provide detailed plans of stock levels and communicate this information to the merchandise teams. One of the most important functions covered by a senior merchandiser or merchandise director is agreeing 'mark downs'. All commercial fashion companies are likely to reduce their unsold stock before the end of the season. Merchandisers need to be commercially aware and have good numeracy skills. Working primarily with databases and spreadsheets, merchandisers need accomplished computer skills and the ability to communicate effectively with internal and external partners. Across the fashion industry, good merchandisers are highly valued for their ability to contribute to the profitability of a fashion organization.

VISUAL MERCHANDISER

Visual merchandising involves the layout and display of merchandise within a defined selling space. The role offers a creative outlet for team-players with practical styling skills and an understanding of how to promote goods and services in keeping with the character and style of a retailer, design label or brand. Visual merchandisers work as part of a team that may be led by a visual merchandising manager, working with senior, head office retail managers or a marketing team. They also liaise closely with merchandisers and buyers. Visual merchandising teams must plan ahead to prepare recurring seasonal themes and specific themes or promotions.

One of the most defining aspects of a visual merchandising role is the installation and maintenance of window displays, which requires a combination of flair and an understanding of the personality of the brand or designer label. Department stores such as Barneys and Selfridges have become acclaimed for their inventive window displays. Other labels, such as Ralph Lauren, are known for their 'lifestyle spaces', where the sales merchandise is seamlessly mixed with antiques or pieces that are painstakingly sourced and arranged to create an alluring retail environment.

Many companies employ in-house visual merchandisers. They should be trend-aware and possess practical skills, creative flair and the ability to show initiative and work within a team.

01 — VISUAL MERCHANDISING
Visual merchandising offers a customer the first impression of a collection within a retail environment. Online shopping has seen visual merchandising transfer to digital formats including the use of virtual models.
Credit: A. Ciampi

01

TEACHING FASHION DESIGN

Fashion design offers a range of teaching opportunities and career paths for individuals with appropriate skills, relevant experience and accomplished communication skills. Taking account of the diverse job roles and career paths that exist across the fashion industry, it is important to understand contemporary practices in relation to one or more specialist subject areas. This might include teaching how to design and research a collection or how to cut patterns or drape in a sample room in order to create prototype samples.

The level of teaching will also vary; it could include teaching fashion design to undergraduate students or working with masters students who will have a prior knowledge and experience of the subject. It is important to be able to recognize the level of the student in order to fully prepare and deliver teaching instruction. In most institutions the link between teaching and learning is recognized; incoming students will often need more skills-led teaching to equip them with the basic competencies on which to build, while more advanced students will be encouraged to test and refine their individual approach towards established practices and conventions in order to develop their learning independence and define their personal style as designers or creative practitioners.

Some fashion instructors teach on a factional basis. This means that they do not work full-time at a university or college, choosing instead to maintain their own practice or consultancy work. In this way, some instructors maintain and reinforce their links with the fashion industry. This helps to keep their practice contemporary and industry-relevant while informing their teaching practice for the benefits of the students. Full-time teaching instructors will also engage in research or scholarship activities to ensure that their knowledge of the fashion subject area and its evolving practices remains current and relevant.

Teaching fashion design requires a high level of planning and organizational skills to support and nurture individual student talent and ambition. Working as part of a team, a fashion design tutor's contribution will be defined through a teaching schedule or timetable. Student groups will vary in size and access to equipment and resources, including sample room facilities, will usually be well maintained and supported through a programme of regular investment.

Teaching activities may include any of the following:

Preparing a structured syllabus over a defined number of weeks with learning and teaching objectives appropriate to the level of the student group

Planning and writing relevant projects. This might include collaborative projects with external contacts or professional bodies

Planning and delivering a series of practical workshops or studio-based activities

Planning and delivering presentations or lectures to student groups

Organizing a study visit to an appropriate destination. This might include a visit to an exhibition or trade event

Arranging for a guest speaker or industry contacts to support a teaching session or project by delivering a presentation or workshop

Directly supervising and guiding students within a supportive learning environment

01

01–02__ TEACHING FASHION

Fashion students often present their samples to tutors for feedback and advice. This may take the form of a critique in the company of their peers. Such occasions enable students to articulate their ideas and reflect on feedback.
Credit: Alick Cotterill

02

Q&A
Marcella L

Name

Marcella L

Occupation

Fashion blogger

Website

www.fashiondistraction.com

Biography

Marcella is a 23-year-old blogger based in Auckland, New Zealand. She recently finished a double degree at the University of Auckland, majoring in Economics and Statistics. Marcella started Fashion Distraction in 2008 as a side project to her store, but it has evolved over the years.

Please introduce us to your blog Fashion Distraction; what do you cover and why did you start your own blog?

Originally I was only taking pictures of myself to sell clothes online, but I found I really enjoyed putting together outfits and I ended up with a lot of looks that I liked so I wanted an outlet to document them all. Then I discovered the whole blogosphere community and decided to try it out myself, and it just went from there. Now my site has evolved into an extensive photo diary of my day-to-day outfits, inspirations and snapshots from my daily lifestyle.

Can you tell us about your personal style and the 'shop my closet' section?

I'm a bit of a chameleon, I don't really have a definable style or look per se, I just like to take items which catch my interest and build an outfit around it. Some days I'll dress girly, other times edgy, vintage or even quirky.

As for my blogshop, basically, my closet went way beyond the point of full capacity, and I'm trying to tidy up the damage by doing a huge clean out of items I no longer want, or still do but just never get the chance to wear. It's a natural extension of my blog I guess: if girls who follow my blog like my style, then chances are they might be interested in the pieces I'm selling from my own closet.

I see that you also use Facebook and Twitter; how do they complement your blog?

Facebook and Twitter are a great way to get instant updates to my followers. I'll put a link to my latest post as well putting up previews of upcoming content. It's a great way of starting up a conversation with some of my readers, getting feedback about what they like and what they want to see more of, and answering some of their questions as well.

Tell use about your interest in photography and where you get the inspiration for your photoshoots

I'm really lucky that my boyfriend and I developed an interest in photography together as he started taking more and more photos for my blog. He invested in the equipment and just taught himself all the technical knowledge along the way, while we worked on the creative side together by studying and appreciating magazine editorials and looking at other blogs. I'm really proud of how far the photos on the blog have come, although we are constantly still trying to improve and learn more as we go.

What advice would you offer to an aspiring fashion blogger?

Make your content original and attractive – just be yourself and develop your own style rather than trying to emulate anyone else. You have to be prepared to be patient and keep at it, success doesn't happen overnight. Most importantly, though, have fun with it, and don't take it too seriously at the end of the day, you should be blogging to enjoy it.

Where do you see Fashion Distraction heading in the coming years?

Hopefully still going strong but managing to keep it fresh at the same time. I would like to perhaps build it up to something a little more professional-looking over time but for the most part, I'm quite happy with the look and feel of the site as it is now.

01

01—02 __ FASHION DISTRACTION
Marcella's blog has evolved into an extensive photo diary of day-to-day outfits, inspirations and snapshots.
Credit: Fashion Distraction / photos by Jared Belle

6.0 PORTFOLIO AND PROFESSIONAL PRACTICE

02

7/11/2011
slouch.

The 'Vanda' bag, available HERE

The perfect boho bag.

Like 8   Tweet
· BAGS_MI PIACI

«Prev 1 2 3 4 5 6 7 8 9 10 11 Next»

01

01—02 _ BLOGGING
Marcella's advice to potential fashion bloggers is to be patient and keep at it, success doesn't happen overnight.
Credit: Fashion Distraction / photos by Jared Belle

02

6.0 PORTFOLIO AND PROFESSIONAL PRACTICE

Discussion questions
Activities
Further reading

DISCUSSION QUESTIONS

ACTIVITIES

DISCUSSION QUESTIONS

1 Discuss areas of good practice in relation to fashion portfolios. Consider what makes an effective fashion portfolio. How many projects should you include? How should you edit and update your portfolio?

2 Evaluate the impact and diversity of technology-enabled platforms for self-marketing and personal promotion including e-portfolios, blogs and personal websites. Discuss their benefits and limitations for fashion designers.

3 Referring to the career opportunities outlined in this chapter, discuss the role of a fashion designer and their working relationship with associated professionals.

ACTIVITIES

1 Review your portfolio. Critically evaluate your personal strengths and areas for improvement. Edit and update your work with reference to market and customer focus, presentation formats and the overall organization of your work. Prepare a supplementary lookbook for your final/senior collection using styled photographs of your work.

2 Identify a variety of fashion and lifestyle blogs including personal and corporate blogs. Evaluate their content and features. Create your own blog and include a variety of text and images. Add your own links and settings and update your content. Review your blog at regular intervals.

3 Prepare a CV/resumé with a covering letter to accompany your portfolio. Use a simple, legible font and include your contact details, education profile, summary of skills, any honours or awards, internships and any proposed references to be contacted. Draft a covering letter outlining your personal strengths and tailor this to your intended application.

FURTHER READING

The only profit
centre is the
customer. **PETER F. DRUCKER**

Brown, C
**Fashion & Textiles: The
Essential Careers Guide**
Laurence King, 2010

Davies, H and Knight, N
British Fashion Designers
Laurence King, 2009

Davies, H
Modern Menswear
Laurence King, 2008

Editors of Nylon
**Street: The 'Nylon' Book
of Global Style**
Universe Publishing, 2006

Finnan, S
**How To Prepare For A
Career In Fashion:
Fashion Careers Clinic
Guide**
Adelita, 2010

Goworek, H
**Careers in Fashion and
Textiles**
John Wiley & Sons, 2006

Jaeger, A
**Fashion Makers Fashion
Shapers: The Essential
Guide to Fashion by
Those in the Know**
Thames & Hudson, 2009

Rodic, Y
Facehunter
Thames & Hudson, 2010

Schuman, S
The Sartorialist
Penguin, 2009

Tain, L
**Portfolio Presentation
for Fashion Designers**
Fairchild, 2004

Verle, S
**Style Diaries: World
Fashion from Berlin to
Tokyo**
Prestel, 2010

Arts Thread
www.artsthread.com

Facehunter
**www.facehunter.
blogspot.com**

Fashion Snoops
www.fashionsnoops.com

Flickr
www.flickr.com

LOOKBOOK.nu
www.lookbook.nu

Not just a label
www.notjustalabel.com

SHOWstudio
www.showstudio.com

Stylebubble
**www.stylebubble.
typepad.com**

Stylesightings:
www.stylesightings.com

WGSN
www.wgsn.com

The September Issue
DVD, 2009

CONCLUSION

Fashion design accommodates a diverse range of contexts, ideas and practices that are essentially linked to human criteria. The appeal of fashion may be attributed to its ability to transcend and even embrace opposing forces and influences by applying a transient significance to human appearance and identity.

In recent years the fashion industry has witnessed the inexorable rise and influence of new technologies. While many of these technological advances are taking place outside the sample rooms or ateliers of fashion houses, their impact is having a very real effect on fashion consumer expectations and buying behaviour. The development of information communication channels, including websites, blogs, live streaming of fashion shows, and the growth of social media sites and smart phone apps, have made fashion design ever more accessible to an international marketplace; the industry operates in realtime whenever and wherever you may be. Consumers today are even invited to participate in the design process, with brands using technology-enabled websites to offer personalization and customization services. In addition, fashion design continues to be driven by a wider social agenda and an impetus to improve its public image either through developing sustainable business models and traceable supply chains or by association with good causes and ethical practices that empower consumers and benefit suppliers and workers.

As fashion continues to define and redefine itself, with designers examining its past, presenting a view of modernity and expressing contemporary tastes and values, it becomes clear that fashion is also shaped by its human relationships and organizational structures.

For a designer, fashion offers personal expression, social interaction and communities. Building and sustaining a career as a fashion designer requires clarity of purpose supported by an underlying philosophy and effective communication and inter-personal skills. Fashion challenges designers to reconcile their ideas and aspirations with critical processes and practices that must ultimately address the human form. Central to this critical path is an appreciation for fabrics and their application to the body in the formation and development of a prototype sample. It is one of the marvels of the design process that, within this seemingly constrained framework, designers continue to surprise and excite audiences with evolutionary and sometimes radical designs, expressed through a seemingly infinite variety of shapes, lines, colours and proportions season upon season.

APPENDIX

Index

Page numbers in italic refer to captions

**Index compiled by
Ursula Caffrey**

Acknowledgements

I would like to thank all the contributors who so generously provided original material for this book. In alphabetical order: Emma Brown, Mayya Cherepova, Anne Combaz, Catherine Corcier, Alick Cotterill, Mengjie Di, Mei Dyke, Lisa Galesloot, HollyMae Gooch, Hanyuan Guo, Katharine Nelson, Lauren Sanins, Laura Helen Searle, Shijing Tuan, Kate Wallis and Kun Yang.

Special thanks to my contributors who agreed to be interviewed for this book: Marcella L, Lee Lapthorne, Daria Lipatova, Maggie Norris, Lauretta Roberts and Damien Shaw. Additional thanks also to Olivia Chen, Chip Harris, Sachiko Honda, Cecilia Langemar, Wendy Turner, Rui Yang and Alison Wescott for their assistance.

Thank you to catwalking.com and everyone at AVA Publishing, especially Rachel Parkinson, and to Violetta Boxill at Alexander Boxill.

Credits

CHAPTER 1.0

009	Anne Combaz
011	Catwalking
013	Anne Combaz for *Tush* magazine
019	Catwalking
022-023	Shutterstock
031	Farrukh Younus @Implausibleblog
032-033	Shutterstock
034	PF / Keystone USA / Rex Features
035	Courtesy of SOKO
037-039	Lee Lapthorne

CHAPTER 2.0

043	Mengjie Di
045	Mengjie Di
047	Alick Cotterill
049	Alick Cotterill
051	Hanyuan Guo
052-054	HollyMae Gooch
055	Mengjie Di
056	Mengjie Di
057	HollyMae Gooch
058	Shijing Juan
059	HollyMae Gooch
060	Laura Helen Searle www.laurahelensearle.com
061	Catherine Corcier
063	Mengjie Di
064	Mengjie Di
065	Daria Lipatova
066	Kun Yang
067	Shijing Tuan
068	Laura Helen Searle www.laurahelensearle.com
071-073	Daria Lipatova

CHAPTER 3.0

077	Totem / Ugo Camera
081	Catwalking
082	Emma Brown
085	Mayya Cherepova
086	Catwalking
087	Messe Frankfurt Exhibition GmbH / Pietro Sutera
088-089	Lauren Sanins
091	01: JB Spector / Museum of Science and Industry 02: Lisa Galesloot
093-095	Messe Frankfurt Exhibition GmbH
099	Messe Frankfurt Exhibition GmbH / Pietro Sutera
100-101	Remi
103-105	WGSN

CHAPTER 4.0

109	Laura Helen Searle www.laurahelensearle.com
111	Alison Westcott
113	Penny Brown
119	Laura Helen Searle www.laurahelensearle.com
120-121	Penny Brown
125	Laura Helen Searle www.laurahelensearle.com
127	Lauren Sanins
128-129	Penny Brown
133	Tsolmandakh Munkhuu / Totem
135-137	Maggie Norris Couture

CHAPTER 5.0

141	Lisa Galesloot
143	Anne Combaz
144	Kate Wallis
145	Anne Combaz
146	Kate Wallis
147	Lauren Sanins
148	Anne Combaz
149	Wayne Tippetts / Rex Features
150	Ethel Davies / Robert Harding / Rex Features
151	Catwalking
153	Kate Wallis
154	Hanyuan Guo
156-157	Lisa Galesloot
159	01: Mei Dyke 02: Mayya Cherepova
161	Lisa Galesloot
162	Lisa Galesloot
164-165	Catwalking
167	Catwalking
168	Ed Reeve / View Pictures / Rex Features
169	Catwalking

CHAPTER 6.0

173	Autumn de Wilde / Rodarte
179	Katharine Nelson
180	Nils Jorgensen / Rex Features
183	Philip Hollis / Rex Features
185	Craig Lawrence / Totem
187	01: Ray Tang / Rex Features 02: Shutterstock
189	AGF s.r.l. / Rex Features
191	Breadandbutter.com
193	A. Ciampi / Pitti Immagine
195	Alick Cotterill
197-199	Fashion Distraction / photos by Jared Belle